THE
OWNER-BUILT
ADOBE HOUSE

THE
OWNER-BUILT
ADOBE HOUSE

Duane Newcomb

University of New Mexico Press
Albuquerque

The Owner-Built Adobe House was originally published by
Charles Scribner's Sons in 1980, ISBN 0-684-16609-7.
University of New Mexico Press paperbound edition
published 2001 by arrangement with the author.

Library of Congress Cataloging-in-Publication Data

Newcomb, Duane G.
    The owner-built adobe house / Duane Newcomb.
        p. cm.
    Originally published: New York : Scribner, c1980.
    Includes bibliographical references and index.
    ISBN 0-8263-2323-5 (paper : alk. paper)
        1. Adobe houses—Design and construction—Amateurs' manuals.
I. Title.

TH4818.A3 N48 2001
693'.22—dc21

                                                00-069781

---

*To people everywhere
who would like to build a better house
for less money.*

Contents

Introduction   1

1 Selecting a Site for Your Adobe House   4

Making Sure Your Site Has Water Potential   4
Checking for Adequate Septic Tank Percolation   7
Checking on Power and Telephone Lines   9
Examining the Feasibility of Future Access Roads   10
Checking the Clay Content of the Soil   11
Checking Local Zoning Laws   13
Checking the Title   14
Evaluating the Terrain and Site Features   16
Making Sure You Are Getting Your Money's Worth   16

2 Planning Your Adobe House   18

Planning the Interior   20
Drawing Up Plans   30
Obtaining Permits   34

3 Making Adobe Bricks   35

Uniform Building Code Requirements   36
Testing the Stabilized Bricks   37
Making Your Adobe Molds   40
Starting Production   42

4 Preparing and Building the Foundation   49

Excavating the Site   49
Corner Staking the House   50

Digging the Footings   52
Pouring the Concrete Slab   56
Framing the Floor   57

5 Putting Up Adobe Walls   60

Getting Your Equipment Together   60
Mixing Mortar   60
Laying Adobe Bricks Properly   61
Allowing for Doors and Windows   63
Bond Beams and Lintels   65
Steel Reinforcing   66
Post Adobe Construction   68

6 Installing the Plumbing System   77

The Drainage System   77
The Water Supply System   84
Installing Your Fixtures   87
The Septic System   88

7 Installing Electrical Wiring   90

Planning the Electrical System   90
Selecting Wire and Boxes   91
Wiring Circuits and Installing Boxes   93
Wiring Heavy-Duty Appliances   99
Installing the Service Panel   102
Testing and Labeling the Circuits   104

8 Heating and Cooling Your House   106

Forced-Air Central Heating   106
Radiant Heating   112
Solar Heating   114
Cooling an Adobe House   115

9 Building Your Adobe Fireplace   117

Types of Fireplaces   117
Designing Your Fireplace   119
Building Your Fireplace   120
Circulating Fireplaces   126

10 Framing and Covering the Roof   127

Putting the Roof Plan on Paper   128
Framing the Roof   130
Covering the Roof   136

11   Finishing the Exterior and Interior   141

    Applying Plaster   141
    Plastering the Interior   142
    Installing Drywall   143
    Selecting and Hanging Doors   144
    Installing the Windows   148
    Installing Kitchen Cabinets   150
    Selecting and Installing Floor Covering   151
    Adding the Trim   153

Bibliography   155
Index   157

THE
OWNER-BUILT
ADOBE HOUSE

Introduction

I originally decided to build my first post adobe house simply because I didn't want to pay $70,000 to $100,000 for a home or be stuck with unrealistic high monthly payments.

After talking to a few builder friends and doing a little research, I began to realize that the only way I could have the house I wanted at a price I could afford would be to cut labor costs drastically by doing most of the work myself and by substituting some low-cost building materials for the traditional higher-priced materials used in most houses.

Since I lived in California I had long been aware of the old missions and other historic buildings built with adobe. I had also been in some very modern, very livable adobe houses where the owners had made the adobe bricks at little cost from the soil right on the site.

Some of the adobe houses I saw at that time had been built for $20,000, $15,000, $10,000, and less. Yet these same houses built from adobe by traditional construction methods would have cost $80,000 to $150,000 and more.

Without a doubt, this was for me!

Three weeks later I purchased 5½ acres with a $2,000 down payment and made up my mind to build an adobe house.

At that time I knew absolutely nothing about building a house and even less about adobe. But I found all the information I needed to make adobe bricks in *Making the Adobe Brick* by Eugene Boudreau (see Bibliography). With the help of this book I proceeded to make 7,000 bricks.

After that, I began to build a nine-room, 2,700 square foot post adobe house. By reading and by asking the advice of local building supply dealers, I managed to lay bricks, frame the interior walls, install the heating system, do most of my own plumbing and wiring, shingle the roof, and solve other problems as they came up.

When I was finished, I had spent a total of about $20,000, excluding the cost of the land. This money came from savings and from income acquired as I went along. Currently, this same house is worth more than $130,000.

In the course of building I discovered that adobe is a material that takes on a form and a character all its own and that working with adobe is an experience unlike any other. The best part, however, is that adobe is probably the only building material left today that is almost free, and building with it is certainly the only method left in which you can start with little cash and wind up with an expensive custom house.

Most people, of course, consider adobe to be primarily a product of the Southwest, but using today's modern stabilization techniques and the proper soil, you can build with adobe almost anywhere in the United States.

In building my own first post adobe and in working with adobe since completing that house, I have become increasingly aware that there is very little information available on adobe construction techniques that will show you how to do all the work yourself.

That's what this book is all about. It is designed so you can start with absolutely no experience and handle all the phases of building an adobe house with a minimum of difficulty.

In doing your own building you have many options. You can, for instance, make all the bricks yourself, or purchase them ready-made. You can do your own wiring, plumbing, roofing, and other tasks or choose the ones you wish to do and hire subcontractors to handle the rest. In addition, you can make all sorts of material substitutions to cut costs even further. Some owner-builders tear down old buildings just to get the lumber, and others scrounge for scraps;

one owner-builder I know obtained permission from the local power company to tear down an old trestle on their property to obtain timbers that eventually became posts and headers in his post adobe house. Still others buy second-hand windows and doors from dealers who specialize in this type of merchandise. There are many possibilities.

I have dedicated this book to people who would like to build a better house for less money. If that's you, I hope you'll try adobe. When you finish, you can take pride in the house that you built with your own hands.

1

Selecting a Site for Your Adobe House

Property selection should be both fun and serious business. It is at this stage that you are going to eliminate the problems that might well cost you thousands of dollars later on. On one western site, for instance, the owners built their home, then drilled 200 feet twice for water and came up dry both times. In California a couple purchased several acres of land only to discover the county wouldn't let them build because the property wasn't suitable for a septic tank. And in Arkansas, when the owner started to build he discovered that the power company wanted to charge him $15,000 just to bring electricity to the property.

When you begin to look for a site on which to build your adobe house, you should not only look for a good location but you should also consider a number of other practical factors that can sometimes make the difference between building or not building on a particular piece of property.

MAKING SURE YOUR SITE HAS WATER POTENTIAL

If you buy a city lot, you will probably find that a public or private agency already supplies water directly to your lot. If you buy acreage, a water company or agency may or may not provide service. To find out about an already existing local water supply ask the real estate agent who listed the property. When you get an answer double-check the information with the neighbors.

In my own case I bought land from a retired real estate developer who had subdivided an 80 acre ranch. The agent-developer told me that all property owners owned a portion of an existing iron-pipe irrigation system. It turned out that the system had actually been purchased by a county water agency, and that agency now charged $80 a year for the water. In addition the water was untreated and could not be used for drinking purposes unless an $800 filter system was installed.

Local water agencies or water companies make the best sources for information about water systems. You will usually find them listed in the phone book. If they service your property, find out the distance you will be required to extend your own pipe to connect with the existing water source and whether or not you can use the water for domestic purposes. Installing a filter system or running pipe long distances will add to the cost of developing the property.

If you cannot connect with an existing water source, you will have to generate a good water supply on your own land. You can usually convert a small surface spring into a usable water supply by storing the water in some type of tank. If you have any doubts about whether the spring is safe for drinking, have the water tested by a commercial laboratory. You will find these listed in the Yellow Pages under "Laboratories." Labs test for the presence or absence of coliform-type bacteria. The maximum acceptable count for most health departments is one coliform-type bacterium per 100 cubic centimeters of water. This type of bacteria will not harm humans, but its existence in a water supply indicates that harmful intestinal bacteria may be present. In some areas the local county health department will test your water supply free.

If you find an existing well on your property, check it out before deciding that it will make a good water supply. Ask the seller whether the well provides water year-round. Then ask the nearest neighbors what they know.

Next check the flow rate of the well. A well should flow at a minimum rate of 2 to 2½ gallons (7.6–9.5 L) per minute. If the water seems to flow slowly into an existing well, test the gallon-per-minute rate this way: Pump the well dry, then turn off the pump for five minutes to allow more water to enter the well. Start the pump and direct the flow into a 5 gallon (19 L) bucket. When the bucket fills up, dump it out and start again. Keep this up until the pump sucks air. This will give you a rough idea of how many gallons of water per minute the well will yield.

For instance, if you fill the 5 gallon bucket twice before the pump starts to suck air, then 10 gallons (38 L) of water has run into the well in the five-minute period, for a flow rate of 2 gallons (8 L) per minute.

If you find that you need to drill a new well, you will have to make an educated guess as to whether or not you have water on the property and what it will cost to develop it as a source. Unfortunately, it is difficult for an untrained eye to tell if water exists under a particular piece of property.

The U.S. Geological Survey, the State Board of Water Resources, and other government agencies have prepared reports on the ground-water potential of many areas. These reports are often available at the local library. You can also ask a geologist (found in the Yellow Pages) to study the rock formations and to give you an opinion about the chances of finding water. For this service you can expect to pay $100 to $200.

Often, local commercial well-drillers can give you an idea of whether you are likely to find water. Unfortunately, they are not always accurate. Commercial well-drillers will also sometimes tell you that water is "probably" available when they don't really know whether it is there or not.

Finally, plants and trees indicate the presence of water. These plants can be especially useful if you intend to drill your own well rather than hire a commercial well-driller to drill it for you.

Some Plants Indicating Water

Plant	Water Depth
Cottontails or rushes	Near surface
Cottonwood trees	10–30 ft (3–10 m)
Elderberry	10–15 ft (3–5 m)
Greasewood	10–30 ft (3–10 m)
Mesquite	10–40 ft (3–12 m)

While you cannot always tell if water exists before you drill, you can sometimes hedge. Some commercial well-drillers, for instance, advertise "No Water, No Pay." While they usually charge a little more than other commercial well-drillers, they may be worth the added expense if you are unsure that water even exists on the property.

In addition, sometimes you can purchase property with the condition that you must find good water within 200 feet (61 m) of the surface. Also a few local laws now insist that developers put in a usable well before they sell the property.

CHECKING FOR ADEQUATE SEPTIC TANK PERCOLATION

In the past, some owner-builders installed inadequate septic systems that overflowed in rainy weather or contaminated the water supply because of their location. Now, however, county health departments everywhere have severely tightened the rules for allowing septic tanks on a particular piece of property. Most systems now installed in rural areas consist of a septic tank connected to a disposal field that disperses the liquid and permits the soil bacteria and the ground filtration to remove the pollutants.

As a general rule, a septic system can't be located in a swampy area, where the water table comes within a few feet of the ground surface, or where the disposal field will be flooded part of the year. The disposal field also must be located 100 feet (31 m) away from a well or spring and 50 feet (15 m) away from a lake or stream.

Liquids draining from a septic system must percolate through the soil at the rate of at least 1 inch (2.54 cm) an hour. Sometimes liquids drain at a slower rate because bedrock, hardpan, or an impenetrable soil condition exists under the entire property. In cases like these, the local health department often won't allow you to build. It is important, therefore, that you know if you can install a septic system on a particular piece of property before you purchase that property.

When possible, make the following rule-of-thumb percolation test. This test won't be accepted by most health departments, but it will give you an idea of the conditions existing on that property. Later, when you are ready to build, you can

Absorption Rate Requirements for Private Residences

Percolation Rate (time required for water to fall 1 in. per min)	Required Absorption Area in sq ft per Bedroom Standard Trench and Seepage Pits
1 or less	70 (6.5 sq m)
2	85 (8 sq m)
3	100 (9.3 sq m)
4	115 (10.7 sq m)
5	125 (11.6 sq m)
10	165 (15.3 sq m)
15	190 (17.7 sq m)
30	250 (23 sq m)
45	300 (28 sq m)
60	330 (30.7 sq m)
60 plus	unacceptable

have an official percolation test made by someone licensed to do it. Here is how to make your own pretest.

- Dig or bore a hole 6 to 12 inches (15–30 cm) wide to a depth of about 36 inches (92 cm). Remove the loose material from the hole and place 2 inches (5 cm) of fine gravel on the bottom.

• Fill the hole with water and leave it overnight. If the water immediately sinks into the top layer of soil, fill it again. Next day add water to bring the depth to 1 to 2 inches (2.5–5 cm) above the gravel. Now, using a ruler, measure the drop in the water for the next hour.

A water drop of between 1 inch a minute and 1 inch every thirty minutes is good. A water drop of between 1 inch every thirty minutes and 1 inch every hour is acceptable. If the water in the test hole takes more than one hour to fall 1 inch, this will be unacceptable to most health departments. The actual requirements vary with the area, so check with your local health department.

CHECKING ON POWER AND TELEPHONE LINES

It is surprising how many people assume that both telephone service and power will be available wherever they decide to build. If you build on a city lot, you probably will have power available. But if you intend to build on country acreage, you may have to bring the telephone and power lines a mile or more to your property.

Most companies now charge for bringing power to your site.

If you are considering buying a particular piece of property, first spot the nearest power pole. This will give you a general idea of how far you will have to bring the power. Next ask the neighbors which power and telephone companies serve the area. Call both offices and ask about rates for extending their lines. Some companies maintain representatives who will come out to the property, explain the charges, and try to help as much as possible with information and advice.

Some companies, however, won't extend the lines until they have a certain number of customers in an area. In addition, if several people develop adjacent properties at about the same time, the first one to build sometimes pays the bulk of the cost. In other cases, all property owners share the cost of bringing the power to all lots. The local power company representative can usually help you clarify these situations.

EXAMINING THE FEASIBILITY OF FUTURE ACCESS ROADS

Before you buy land, determine what it will cost to construct an access road. Walk any possible road location first and look for creeks, swampy areas, rock outcrops, and large trees you will need to remove. Now do a little homework. if you need to remove a rock outcrop, obtain an estimate from a blasting contractor (found under "Blasting Contractor's in the Yellow Pages). If you need to cut down trees, ask a local tree service for an estimate, or if you intend to do it yourself, decide on your equipment needs and check rental costs.

You will also need to think about a surface for your road. You can grade it and leave it, but this type of road becomes rutted and slippery in wet weather. Usually, roads are surfaces with crushed rock on a dirt base, with crushed rock on a road-oil base, or with blacktop. You need to decide what you want to do and then estimate costs.

If you intend to grade the road yourself and apply 3 to 4 inches (8–10 cm) of crushed rock, call a local rental operator and obtain tractor rental charges, then call a local sand and gravel firm and ask for the price per cubic yard (.76 cu m) of crushed rock (generally $6 to $10). A 10 foot (3 m) wide road, 100 feet (30 m) long, spread 4 inches (10 cm) deep with crush rock will require approximately 12 cubic yards (9 cu m) of gravel. This will cost $120 for gravel at $10 a cubic yard.

$$10 \text{ ft} \times 100 \text{ ft} = 1{,}000 \text{ sq ft}$$
$$1{,}000 \text{ sq ft} \times 1/3 \text{ ft } (4 \text{ in}) = 333 \text{ cu ft}$$
$$333 \text{ cu ft} \div 27 \text{ cu ft per yard} = 12.3 \text{ cu yd}$$

Estimate other surfaces the same way.

If you intend to hire a contractor to build the road, call several and ask them to give you an estimate. This type of prechecking will take extra time but will give you a good general idea of whether a particular piece of property will fall within your budget requirements.

Besides figuring possible costs, in checking out future roads you will need to look at the deed and make sure that you have an easement across any private property that lies between the property you intend to buy and the public road. More than one property owner has bought land only to find that he or she couldn't gain access because the deed didn't have an easement and the owners of the surrounding property simply didn't want anyone crossing their land. In many cases, however, the original subdivider will have provided an easement. You can check this by looking at the deed in the county recorder's office (this will be covered in more detail later in this chapter).

CHECKING THE CLAY CONTENT OF THE SOIL

Most people who make bricks for their adobe houses want to make those bricks directly from the soil on their own lots. However, the Uniform Building Code says that any soil used in making adobe bricks must have clay content between 25 and 45 percent. Surprisingly, the soil in many areas throughout the United States is perfectly suitable for adobe building. This includes the states of Oregon and Washington, the deep South, and some of the East.

Often you can rule out the soil on a particular piece of property just by looking at it. Extremely sandy soil or dark loamy soil obviously will not make good adobe bricks. Sometimes, however, it is difficult to tell by either feeling the soil with your hands or turning it over with a shovel. If you think the soil on the lot you are considering might be suitable for making adobe bricks, you can perform a simple test with a one-quart glass jar and a soil sample. Here's how to do it.

• Obtain a soil sample from the area where you intend to take your soil. Dig down 2 to 3 feet (.6–.9 m), then mix the soil in the hole to combine the layers.

- Place some of the soil from your sample in a one-quart glass jar. Cover the soil with 3 to 4 inches (8–10 cm) of water and shake. When it is thoroughly mixed let the soil settle.
- Examine the soil layers after they have completely settled. You will find coarse sand and pebbles at the bottom, fine sand and silt next, clay on top, then water (Figure 1).
- Take a ruler and measure from the bottom of the jar to the top of the clay layer. Then measure the depth of the clay layer alone. Determine the percentage of clay in your sample by dividing the total height of the clay column in inches by the total height of the soil column. For example, if the clay column measures 1 inch (2.5 cm) and the total soil column 4 inches (9 cm), then the sample contains 25 percent clay.

If your test shows that your soil contains too much clay (above 45 percent) then you will need to add sand. If your soil contains too little clay you will need to purchase soil with the right clay content. If your self-test indicates a clay content of from 30 to 45 percent, be assured that you can make good bricks from that particular soil.

You can order sand, as well as soil with a high clay content, from a sand and gravel dealer. You will probably want to order a full truckload of soil and have it delivered. Don't mix this soil with your own, however, but make the bricks directly from the imported soil. (At some point during the building process you will need to have your soil tested by a commercial lab, since most building departments require this test before approving your bricks for construction use.)

In practice I have found that self-testing generally indicates a higher clay content in the soil than actually exists. The clay level in the 10-inch glass cookie jar I used for testing indicated a 33 percent clay content. Not satisfied with one test, I ran a total of eight with the same results. I then went ahead and made 500 bricks. When I finally had the soil tested by a commercial lab, their test—the percentage of total material passing through a 200-mesh-per-square-inch screen—showed a clay content of 26 percent. If the results had been

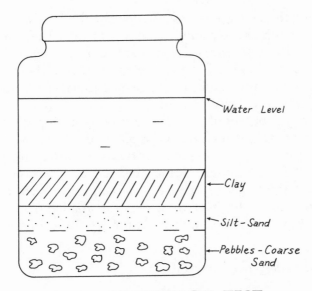

Figure 1. **ADOBE SOIL TEST**

just two percentage points lower I would have been obliged to throw away every last one of my 500 completed bricks.

As a result of this, I recommend that you run a self-test before you buy any property, then have your soil tested by a commercial lab before you start to build bricks.

CHECKING LOCAL ZONING LAWS

When you consider buying a particular piece of property you should visit the county planning department. First obtain a copy of the county (or city) zoning ordinance: Some counties now restrict the subdivision of acreage below 40, 20, 5, or 2½ acres (16, 8, 2, or 1 h). It is important to know what kind of restrictions exist. If, for instance, you intend to buy 5 acres, build on half, and sell half, you will want to know whether or not this is possible. You will also want to know about set-backs. Some ordinances require that the house be set back 30 to 50 feet (9–15 m) from any property lines, but under some conditions you can have this setback waived. If you are buying acreage this probably isn't important. But in several cases

I know of the acreage was so steep that the house had to be built at the top of the property a few feet away from the property line. If the planning department had not been willing to allow a variance, either the adobe couldn't have been built or the site would have had to have been excavated farther down the hill at a much greater cost.

Finally, you should ask the county planning department what freeways and reservoirs are planned for the area. Check to see if the county or the state intends to widen the existing roads in the near future. Sometimes a piece of property will be perfect right now, but when the county or state takes an additional 50 or 100 feet to widen the road ten years from now, it may well make the site extremely undesirable.

CHECKING THE TITLE

The best way to insure that you know about any future problems that may occur on your property is to check the title yourself. The county assessor's office can supply the lot's parcel number, the area in acres, the assessed value, and the market value. The county recorder's office has the deed to the lot along with any recorded encumbrances. And the county tax collector's office can give you the tax rate and inform you of the existence of any delinquent taxes or special assessments.

When checking with the county recorder's office you will first want to know what easements others have across your property. This is the right others have to construct roads, pipelines, ditches, power lines, or anything else across your property. You certainly will want to know if a neighbor can build a road on your lot or if the local water company has the right at some future time to dig up your front lawn.

However, in certain sections of the country the system of recording easements and other encumbrances is so confused that sometimes it is almost impossible to determine what encumbrances exist on the property you intend to buy.

Here are two easements recorded in one California property deed.

An easement affecting the portion of said land and for the purposes stated herein and incidental purposes in favor of Charles

Schubb, for water ditch, recorded February 9, 1886 in book SS of deeds at page 279, the location or route which is not defined—possibly affects that portion of the herein described property lying in the southwest quarter of the northwest quarter of section 4.

Rights as to the use of certain waters and incidental purposes as set forth in an agreement forming Monte Rio pipeline association recorded April 14, 1926 in book 223 of official records at page 193.

In this case, an old California ranch was subdivided. The easements existed somewhere on the ranch, but it was almost impossible to tell where. As a result, the records on each subdivided 5 to 10 acre lot had to mention the old easements.

Although in most cases records like these won't do you much good, they can sometimes warn you of future complications.

In our first recorded easement, the heirs of Charles Schubb might try to construct the ditch, or they might sell the rights to a company who would then attempt to exercise the old easement.

In some cases, the ownership of your water rights may be specified in the deed. But this is not necessarily true. Water rights are a very complicated problem and vary from state to state. The ownership of land does not always impart the rights to the water on the land. A good reference on water rights is the U.S. Geological Survey Circular 347, available from the U.S. Geological Survey, National Center, Reston, Va. 22092.

The deed will also generally state if the timber rights, mineral rights, or hunting rights are held by someone else. If they are, a company might be able to mine or to cut timber on your land. It is fairly common in some areas for the land to be owned by one party and the mineral or other rights to be owned by someone else, so check the deed for this before you buy.

Previous owners of the land may also have placed restrictions or conditions on building and on land use. In some areas where larger parcels have been divided into smaller lots, it is not uncommon to find restrictions in the deed that require prior architectural approval from a builder or homeowner's association before you build. Finally, the deed will show if there is a mortgage on the property, if back taxes are due, and if there are special assessments, attachments, or judgments.

EVALUATING THE TERRAIN AND SITE FEATURES

Some people like to build on flat acreage, others prefer slightly hilly terrain, and still others like the top of a hill or a steep hillside. You will have to make your decision based on your own preferences. It is best to walk any property you are thinking about buying and try to visualize the possible locations for a house. Simply imagine your adobe house sitting there. Does this spot appeal to you? If not, try someplace else.

Also look at the trees and rock outcrops and try to decide how you can build to take advantage of these features. Again, move the house around in your imagination. When you try this exercise with several pieces of property, you often find that one particular lot will make a natural site for your adobe, while the others won't.

MAKING SURE YOU ARE GETTING
YOUR MONEY'S WORTH

There is no foolproof way to make sure you are getting your money's worth on any piece of land, but you should always try to buy property that is suitable for you at as low a price as possible.

When you start to look for acreage or a lot, first send for the United Farm and the Strout Realty catalogs (United Farm Agency, 612 W. 47th S., Kansas City, Mo. 64112; Strout Realty, 521 E. Green St., Pasadena, Calif. 91101). I personally feel that the land listed with these agencies is priced too high, but the catalogs will give you a general idea of what is available and how much you will have to pay.

Next, go to local real estate agents. They also are trying to get the highest possible price, but they can help you be-

Figure 2. A modern adobe home. This 2,700 sq ft adobe house was built by the owner at about ⅓ the cost of a conventional house. The style of this house really sets off the site.

come acquainted with the area and the asking prices of a number of parcels.

To obtain the lowest price you will have to go directly to the seller. Some prospective buyers post ads on the bulletin boards of local service stations and grocery stores and in the local paper. Following is a model of one ad that was very effective.

> Wanted to buy, 5–10 acres with some timber and year round stream in Humboldt County. Will pay $1,000 an acre. Contact: James Thomas, 111 2nd Street, Sacramento, California 95860.

Once you seriously start to consider a particular piece of land, you can go to the county assessor's office and look up what the present owner paid for the land. You can also compare the asking price of the property you are considering with the asking price of nearby parcels. This kind of checking can give you an idea of whether you are making a good buy.

2

Planning Your Adobe House

The very first step in planning any house is to decide exactly what you want and need in a house. In my own case, this planning session turned out to be an eye-opening experience. I had originally decided that I wanted a long, narrow, medium-size house. But after my wife and I considered our real needs, the finished house turned out to be C-shaped, had 9 rooms, and contained 2,700 square feet of space.

Somewhere in the early planning stages you will need to consider what the outside of your house will look like. I like to lay out my rooms first, then decide what exterior style will go best with my particular floor plan.

As a general rule, adobe doesn't lend itself to styles such as Cape Cod, but looks good with almost any informal, one-story plan. In California, a favorite modern adobe style is Western Ranch combined with large open rooms, open beams, and lots of glass.

Today in New Mexico and Arizona you find many people building what could be called "traditional" adobe homes (Figure 3). The most popular of these are Spanish Colonial (a house designed like a fortress with large masses of wall and one entrance), Territorial (a flat-roofed house with burnt-brick coping at the top of the walls), Pueblo Adobe (a copy of the general form used by the Pueblo Indians), and Contemporary Southwest Adobe (this style utilizes a combination of

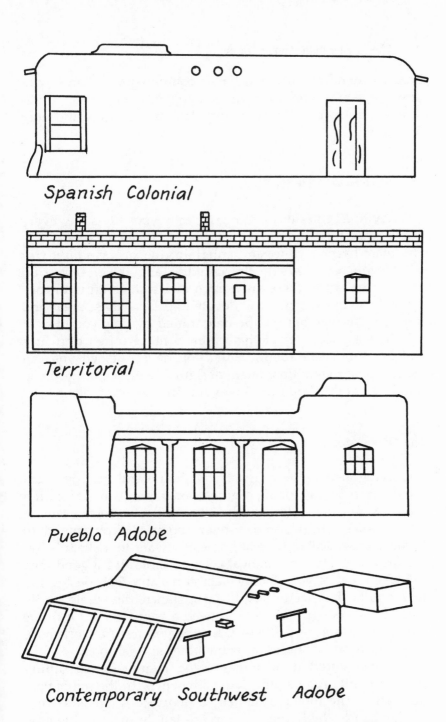

Spanish Colonial

Territorial

Pueblo Adobe

Contemporary Southwest Adobe

Figure 3. **TRADITIONAL SOUTHWEST ADOBES**
(modern versions)

types; generally it has a flat roof combined with large window space and other modern features). Many of these "traditional" Southwest homes feature elaborate window and door detailing.

PLANNING THE INTERIOR

The key to all interior planning is really your life-style. Every house is divided into three major areas: the *living area* where you meet friends, dine, and entertain; the *kitchen-utility area* where you cook and do the laundry; and the *sleeping-bath area*. Secondarily, there are garage and storage areas to consider. How much space you devote to each of these areas and how they fit together will be determined by how you live.

It is a good idea at this point to make rough drawings and notes on each room. When you have finished you can make up a rough floor plan designed with your needs in mind. From this you can draw your final working plans.

The Living Area

The living area is the heart of your home and includes such rooms as a living room, dining room, family or recreation room, game room, den, study, library, music room, sewing room, office, studio, and similar rooms. If you intend to spend a great deal of time at home and want to make this living area as useful and enjoyable as possible, it's a good idea to make a list of your family's activities and then design the rooms to fit those activities. If, for instance, the whole family enjoys Ping-Pong, perhaps you need a game room. Or if one member has a special interest, maybe you need a workshop, a sewing room, a studio, or some other special room.

If you entertain you may want a large formal dining room, a family room, and a large kitchen, with the traffic flow through all the rooms designed so people can circulate from the kitchen to the living room to the family room to the special rooms and back again.

Living Room   In planning your living room, first take into account the general principles that apply to most living rooms.

Your living room can be small, 12 feet by 18 feet (3.7 m x 5.5 m); medium size, 16 feet by 20 feet (5 m x 6 m); or large, 20 feet by 26 feet (6 m x 8 m).

A rectangular room generally makes a better living room than a square room, and the room itself should be located next to the entrance of the house, but the entrance should not necessarily lead directly into the living room. You should also plan the openings to the other rooms to leave as much continuous wall space as possible for the placement of furniture.

Next, consider your personal preference: You can have the living room at the front or at the back of the house. The openings to the other rooms can be rectangular or utilize adobe arches. You can have an open-beam ceiling or a conventional one.

Consider also what type of windows you want in the living room, and whether you want a fireplace, a TV area, a specially designed conversation area, or anything else.

Dining Room Dining rooms, like living rooms, should be planned with a few general rules in mind. Dining rooms should be located next to the kitchen and should have an entrance to both the kitchen and the living room.

A small, 10 feet by 12 feet (3 m x 3.7 m) dining room will accommodate a table and four chairs comfortably. A medium-size, 12 feet by 15 feet (3.7 m x 4.6 m) dining room will seat six to eight people and also have room for a buffet, a china closet, and a server. A large, 14 feet by 18 feet (4.3 m x 5.5 m) dining room will accommodate a large dinner party and also have room for several large pieces of furniture.

Some dining rooms are closed off from the other rooms by doors or constricted openings. Some are open to the living room, the kitchen, or both. Others are a part of the living room, a part of the kitchen, or are separated from the kitchen by a counter or pass-through.

Design your dining room with your likes and dislikes in mind. A good way to do this is to visit some model homes, sit in several different types of dining rooms, and see how they "feel" to you.

Family Room-Recreation Room Most people today want a separate room where the family can work or play. You can use this room as a family room, a TV room, a sewing room, a children's playroom, a hobby room, or almost anything else.

The family room is frequently located next to the kitchen. However, many people prefer the family room next to the living-dining area where it becomes an extension of these rooms for entertaining. Others like it near the living-dining area but closed off so the clutter won't be visible to guests. If you have teenagers, you will want to consider placing this room in some other part of the house so the teenagers can have it completely to themselves.

Most family rooms have dimensions of 12 feet by 16 feet (3.7 m x 5 m), 14 feet by 20 feet (4.3 m x 6 m), or some similar proportions.

If you use the family room extensively for conversation or TV-watching you may also want to add a game room for Ping-Pong, pool, or other activities.

Extra Room: Den, Library, Office   In my own house, I don't think I will ever be without an extra room. Actually I built an office at one end of the house for work, but I also built a separate room near the living room where I can escape the noise and confusion but still feel like part of the family. This extra room may be used as a den, a library, a reading room, a music room, an office, or whatever you prefer.

The Front Entrance   The front entrance should be built close to the living room but apart from it. It should be large enough to hold several people, yet deep enough so that you can walk around an open door. It should also include a small closet. For a front entry 6 feet by 6 feet (1.8 m x 1.8 m) is generally the minimum size, 8 feet by 10 feet (2.4 m x 3.1 m) is average, and 8 feet by 15 feet (2.4 m x 4.6 m) is large.

The Fireplace   Fireplace planning is discussed in detail in Chapter 9.

The guide on the next page is intended to help with your planning. First go over it with your needs in mind, then add anything extra you want to include in your own living area.

The Kitchen-Utility Area

Some families like a lot of space in the kitchen both for cooking and for family activities; this makes the room more of a family social center. Others like to confine the kitchen activities to cooking and eating.

Generally, kitchens are small, 7 feet by 8 feet (2 m x 2.5

Living Area Planning Guide

Rooms
Living room
Dining room
Family room
Game room
Extra room: den, office,
    library, other

General Room Style
Open plan
Closed plan
Open-beam ceilings
Conventional ceilings

Living Room
Small (12' x 18')
Medium (16' x 20')
Large (20' x 26')

Open to other rooms
Closed to other rooms

Front of house
Back of house

Windows: size, type

Floor coverings

Dining Room
Small (10' x 12')
Medium (12' x 15')
Large (14' x 18')

Formal
Open

Part of living room
Part of kitchen
Counter or pass-through

Family Room-Recreational Room
Small (12' x 16')
Medium (14' x 21')
Large (18' x 26')

Family room
Game room
Combination

Open to living-dining rooms
Part of living room
Part of kitchen
In separate part of house

Extra Room
Den, library, office, music
    room, studio, other

Small (8' x 10')
Medium (10' x 12')
Large (14' x 16')

Closet
Special effects

Front Entrance
Small (6' x 6')
Medium (10' x 12')
Large (14' x 16')

Closet
Other

Fireplace
Opening: small, medium, large
Open: 1 side, 2 sides, 3 sides

Rectangular
Adobe arch

Facing: entire wall, partial wall
Other

m); medium, 10 feet by 15 feet (3 m x 4.6 m); or large-family type, 15 feet by 15 feet (4.6 m x 4.6 m), or larger.

The kitchen should be planned so that family traffic stays out of the work area. There should be plenty of counter space, storage space, and electrical outlets. Working counters should be generally 36 inches (91 cm) high, with working table heights of 30 inches (76 cm). You should separate the oven-range from the refrigerator by at least one cabinet, and the doors on all appliances should swing away from the work area.

Now, let's look at a few possible kitchen arrangements (Figure 4).

The U-shaped kitchen has a sink located at the bottom of the U and the range and refrigerator located in either arm. Through-kitchen traffic is automatically kept out of the work area.

The peninsula kitchen is designed in the shape of an F, with the short arm of the F making the peninsula. Quite often this arrangement is used effectively to join the kitchen to the dining room or to the family room.

The L-shaped kitchen usually has a refrigerator in one arm of the L, an oven-range in the other. This arrangement leaves a lot of open space in the kitchen that can be used for dining or as a family area.

The corridor kitchen consists of two parallel corridors with the range top on one side, the refrigerator on the other. This is an efficient plan for a long, narrow room. The disadvantage is that all the kitchen traffic must pass through the work area.

The one-wall kitchen is excellent for a small house, since it takes up very little space. If the kitchen wall is too long, however, cooking requires extra steps.

The island kitchen consists of a central island accessible on all sides. Generally the island contains a sink, a range, or both. The counters, cabinets, and refrigerator occupy the wall space. The island itself can be built in almost any size or shape you desire.

In many homes the utility room is used primarily for washing, drying, and storage, but you can make it big enough to iron or sew there and even include a pantry and extra storage if you like.

A basic utility room should include storage shelves, a

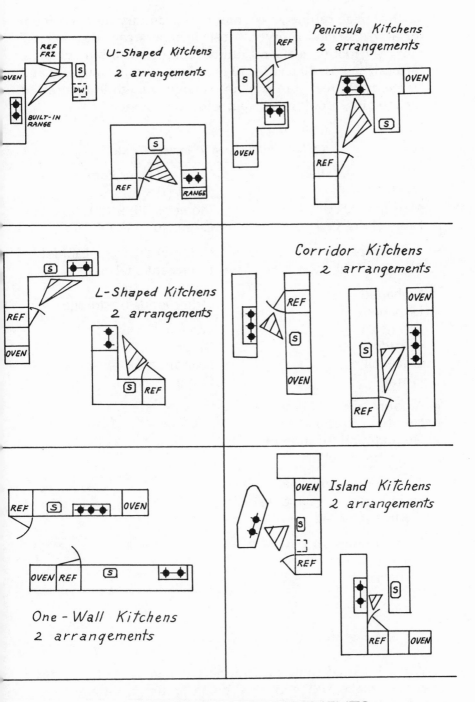

Figure 4. **KITCHEN ARRANGEMENTS**

small storage cabinet, a counter top, a laundry tub, and room for a washer and a dryer. Most designers consider that a 7 foot by 7 foot (2 m x 2 m) utility room is small but adequate for basic needs, 10 feet by 10 feet (3 m x 3 m) is average, and 10 feet by 12 feet (3 m x 3.7 m) is large enough to be utilized for washing, ironing, sewing, and extra storage.

Kitchen-Utility Area Planning Guide

Kitchen	Utility Room
Small (7' x 8')	Small (7' x 7')
Medium (10' x 15')	Medium (10' x 10')
Large (15' x 15')	Large (10' x 12')
Family-type	Detergent storage cabinet
Basic work kitchen	Detergent shelves
U-shaped	Pantry
L-shaped	Other kinds of storage
Peninsula	Washer
Corridor	Dryer
One-wall	Laundry tubs
Island	Other
Amount of counter space	
Number of cabinets	
Number and location of electrical outlets	
Double or single sink	
Sink: ceramic, stainless steel; white, colored	
Type of range and oven	
Garbage disposal	
Dishwasher	

The Sleeping Area

When I started building I didn't have any idea how large I should make either the bedrooms or the bathrooms. As a result I built all the bedrooms except the master bedroom much too large and all three bathrooms too small. To avoid this problem, carefully consider how many bedrooms and bathrooms you want, where you want them, and what size you intend to build them.

If only adults will be living in your house and resale value is not of major importance to you, you'll probably want one or two bedrooms at the most. With children, however, you should plan at least three bedrooms and probably four. You might also consider placing the master bedroom in a completely separate wing from the children's bedrooms.

Usually you'll want to make the master bedroom at least 10 feet by 15 feet (3 m x 4.6 m). If you want a lounging area, plan a minimum of 14 feet by 15 feet (4.3 m x 4.6 m); and if you want a separate bedroom-dressing area, plan the master bedroom in the 15 foot by 20 foot (4.6 m x 6 m) range. Other bedrooms usually are at least 10 feet by 10 feet (3 m x 3 m). But if you intend to include a play area, a study nook, or additional work space, build them 10 feet by 15 feet (3 m x 4.6 m) or larger.

As for the bathrooms, most people think the ideal is one bathroom for the master bedroom, one for the other bedrooms, and a general bathroom for guests. If you are building a small house, however, you'll probably want one bathroom located between the bedrooms or easily reached from them. If you are building a three-bedroom house you'll probably want a bath off the master bedroom and a bath between the other two bedrooms or easily reached from either of them.

The minimum size for a bathroom is 4 feet by 5 feet (1.2 m x 1.5 m). However, this is really squeezing for a toilet, lavatory, and shower because the toilet itself needs 24 inches (60 cm) of space between the front of the toilet and the back wall, and 15 inches (38 cm) of space from the center of the toilet bowl to the side wall or to other fixtures. Small baths generally average 30 square feet (28 sq m), medium baths 40 square feet (37 sq m), and large baths 80 square feet (74 sq m).

In the bathroom you can have almost any type of shower or tub that you want. Showers range from a small, basic 2 foot by 2 foot (.6 m x .6 m) unit to a large one-piece fiberglass or ceramic tile shower. Tubs vary from a basic five-foot tub, to a tub/shower arrangement, to fancy sunken ceramic or fiberglass tubs, and anything else in between.

Bathrooms do not have to be sterile. They can have lots of color, light, and space. You may want to combine your bath with a fancy dressing area complete with lots of cabinets and a vanity. You may want wall-to-wall mirrors or even special shelves to hold decorator accessories or plants.

To get an idea of the possibilities, scan magazines, clipping anything that looks interesting. It is also useful to look through bathroom design books and to visit model homes.

Sleeping and Bath Area Planning Guide

Bedrooms	Bathrooms
Small (10' x 10')	Basic (20 sq ft)
Medium (10' x 15')	Small (30 sq ft)
Large (14' x 15')	Medium (40 sq ft)
	Large (80 sq ft)
Master bedroom:	
Small (10' x 15')	Size/type shower
Medium (14' x 15')	Size/type tub
Large (15' x 20')	
	Vanity
Number of bedrooms	Cabinet space
Separate dressing area	Separate dressing area
Separate dressing room	Other
Separate lounging area	

The Garage

You can have a full attached or detached adobe garage, a carport, or no garage at all. If you are building an adobe house you can pour a concrete slab, put up your posts, and build the roof. This will give you an inexpensive carport. Later you can lay bricks and make it a complete garage.

As a rule of thumb you will need 10 to 15 feet (3–4.6 m) of width and 20 to 25 feet (6–7.6 m) of length for each car. Contractors build small single-car garages 11 feet by 19 feet (3.4 m x 5.8 m), large single-car garages 13 feet by 25 feet (4 m x 7.6 m), and "full" single-car garages 16 feet by 25 feet (5 m x 7.6 m). Small double-car garages are 20 feet by 20 feet (6 m x 6 m) and full double-car garages are 25 feet by 25 feet (7.6 m x 7.6 m). A "full" two-car garage gives you room for two cars plus quite a bit of space for extra storage.

Storage

In general, you should provide storage in the room where you intend to use a particular item. In the living room, family room, den, game room, and dining room, for instance, books, tapes, records, and a hifi unit can be stored in wall-to-ceiling units, in a room divider unit, or on free-standing wall shelves. Picture albums, toys, games, and scrapbooks can be kept in built-in wall cabinets, in window seats, or in a divider between two rooms. China and crystal can be displayed in shallow shelves or in an overhanging, open divider between the rooms. Wine racks can be built into the wall between two rooms, into a hall wall, or into a special wine closet. Bookshelves can also be built into any of the room or hall walls, and extra storage can be added with modular storage-cube wall units.

In the kitchen dried foods or canned goods are easily accessible in open floor-to-ceiling shelves, in pantry cabinets, and in special walk-in pantries. Pans and utensils can hang from overhead racks.

In the bedroom clothes can be accommodated in a conventional closet, a walk-in closet, or specially designed wall-to-wall closets. You may also want to utilize headboard shelves for books, a lamp, a radio, and similar items. In a child's room, wall-cube storage, under-the-bed storage units, or free-standing wall shelves are practical.

In the bathroom consider a built-in closet for towels, wall shelves for plant display, and extra wall cabinets; linen closets can be placed in the bathroom or built into the sides or the end of a hall.

In the garage you can store tools on hanging wall racks. Sporting goods and camping equipment can be stored in built-in wall storage units, on an overhead platform extending from the ceiling, or on free-standing wall shelves. And lawn and garden supplies can be stowed away in wall storage cabinets or in some sort of outside wall cabinet.

There are, of course, many other storage combinations. A good idea is to browse through home and garden magazines, making careful notes on anything you feel you can apply to your own home.

Storage Planning Guide

Living Room	*Bedroom*
Built-in floor-to-ceiling shelves	Conventional closets
Free-standing shelves	Special wall-to-wall closets
Wall cabinets	Walk-in closets
Window seats	Head-of-bed storage
Shallow wall shelves	Under-bed storage
Room dividers	
Wall cubes	*Bathroom*
Built-in wine racks	Linen closet
	Extra towel storage
Kitchen	Extra floor cabinets
Standard cabinets	Open shelves
Open shelves	Bathroom closet
Pantry cabinets	
Built-in pantry	*Garage*
Overhead racks	Tool racks
	Built-in shelves
	Storage cabinets
	Free-standing shelves
	Outside wall cabinets
	Overhead storage

DRAWING UP PLANS

Drawing a plan is not as difficult as it may seem. When I started I had almost no idea how to proceed. But I walked into a contractor's office, asked if I could borrow a set of house plans, and began to draw my plans just like theirs. The main thing I kept in mind was to include all the needed detail and to make it clear and simple.

If you own sophisticated architect's tools—good; if not, buy only the least expensive basics: a T-square, a 12-inch, 45° triangle, four or five HB drawing pencils, a soft eraser, an architect's scale, and about ten sheets or a roll of drafting paper.

You will need to make all drawings to scale. The most common scales are 1 inch = 20 feet for the plot plan, ¼ inch = 1 foot for the foundation, floor, and roof plans, and ¾ inch = 1 foot for wall sections.

Improvised Drafting Table

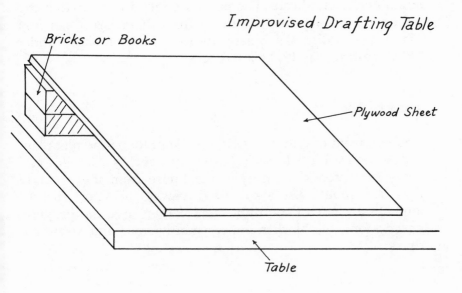

Bricks or Books

Plywood Sheet

Table

Draw Lines With T-Square & Triangle

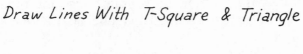

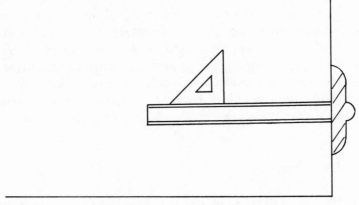

Figure 5. **DRAFTING BASICS**

Most building departments require that drawings be submitted in duplicate. The plans are first drawn on drafting paper, then blueprints are made from them. (You can find places that will make blueprints for you by looking under "Blueprinting" in the Yellow Pages.)

The Plot Plan

You will want to draw the outline of your lot on the plot plan, set the house on it to scale (generally 1 inch = 20 feet), and show the setback distance of the house from the property line. You should also show the driveway and street curb (if any). In a block in the right-hand corner, give the property description: lot, block number, subdivision, and street address.

The Floor Plan

By this stage, you probably already have a rough floor plan along with possible room dimensions. In laying out this floor plan on drafting paper, simply draw your house and rooms to scale (generally ¼ inch = 1 foot). Then label all the rooms and give dimensions.

Now show the location of the plumbing fixtures, the furnace, the water heater, and the fireplace. Draw in all electrical receptacles, switches, light fixtures, and exhaust fans (see Figure 37, page 92, for proper symbols). Label all windows as to size and type. I usually label each window separately on the plan, but some builders include a separate, boxed window schedule that shows the size and type of each window.

Foundation Plan

On the foundation plan draw the outline of your house to scale (¼ inch = 1 foot), then show the footings for the exterior walls, the interior adobe walls, other bearing walls (any wall that helps support the weight of the roof), and the fireplace.

Since adobe is heavier than conventional material, the

foundation of an adobe house must be wider than the foundation of a conventional house. According to the Uniform Building Code the footings should extend beyond the wall by 50 percent. Some local codes allow the footings for adobe walls to extend only 2 to 4 inches (5–10 cm) beyond the wall instead of the full 50 percent. Generally footings must extend 12 to 18 inches (46 cm) below the grade level of the soil.

The footing must be reinforced with ½ inch (1.3 cm) steel rebar that runs the length of the foundation. On the foundation plan you must show a cross section of a typical footing, including the placement of the steel reinforcing rod.

Elevation Sheet

On the elevation sheet show a head-on view of each side of the house. Here you must show the windows, doors, chimneys, porches, and changes in elevation of the roof.

Roof Framing Plan

On the roof framing plan show the joists (the cross members), the rafters, and the ridgeboards. Include cross sections through the roof. Identify all members by size. Some building departments require all members to be identified by species of timber and grade as well as by size. Most building departments will furnish you with a span table, which shows what size the rafters and joists must be. (See also Chapter 10 on roofs.)

If you have wood floors you will also need to include a floor framing plan; see Figure 19, page 58. In addition, if you are building a post adobe house, you will need to include a post adobe framing sheet. See Chapter 5 for details.

Stock Plans You Can Use

I received a great deal of pleasure from designing and drawing the plans for my own house, however, the book *Build with Adobe* by Marcia Southwick (see Bibliography) shows ten floor plans of existing Southwestern adobe houses.

You will also find books of house plans sold on most newsstands. You can write to the addresses listed in the publications for any plans you might like. They are not specifically meant for an adobe house, but in most cases you can modify them to fit your own needs.

Some codes require separate electrical and plumbing/mechanical plans.

OBTAINING PERMITS

Once you have completed your plans, submit them to your local building department. In some states each city and county has a building department. In other states the state handles building permits in rural areas.

When your plans are returned they may have additional requirements noted on the plans. Sometimes everything is included under one permit. In some states, counties, and cities, however, there are separate permits for electrical wiring, gas installation, plumbing, and septic tanks.

In some areas you won't be inspected after you obtain your permit. In other areas you will be required to pass an inspection at every stage. You will be informed of these requirements when you receive your building permit. (For summaries of state and local requirements, see Edmund Vitale, *Building Regulations: A Self-Help Guide for the Owner-Builder*, Charles Scribner's Sons, 1979.)

3
Making Adobe Bricks

Modern adobe bricks consist of a mixture of clay, sand, straw, and emulsified asphalt.

Clay holds your bricks together just like the cement in a concrete block. It contains primarily an aluminum salt and is made up of extremely fine particles. There are several different kinds of clay, but you can use any one of them for making bricks. The so-called adobe soil of the Southwest actually contains too much clay to produce good bricks. What you need is a sandy clay or a clay loam. Soil with too much clay produces too many shrinkage cracks. Soil that is too sandy crumbles easily. As explained in Chapter 1, you can bring in sand or soil with a higher clay content as needed.

Sand, the second ingredient used in making adobe bricks, actually is an inert filler held together by clay, much like gravel in concrete. You can use almost any type of sand in making bricks except beach sand, which contains too much salt. Add extra sand to your soil only when you need to lower the clay content to meet code requirements.

Straw, the third ingredient, doesn't add strength but binds the bricks together and allows them to shrink without cracking.

Emulsified asphalt (a petroleum residue utilized in paving) makes the bricks water-resistant. In ancient days the Babylonians succeeded in making waterproof brick, but the art was lost for centuries—to be rediscovered about fifty years ago. Without the addition of emulsified asphalt, unprotected brick soon weathers away; with it, the bricks stand for many years without appreciable damage.

In New Mexico and nearby areas where the bricks are to be plastered over and not exposed to the weather, they are generally left unstabilized (not treated with emulsified asphalt). Adobe makers create the brick as people have been doing for centuries and simply lay them up in the walls with a mud mortar. You can do this where the codes approve. Bricks exposed directly to the weather must be treated. Cement can also be used as a stabilizer/waterproofer.

UNIFORM BUILDING CODE REQUIREMENTS

The Uniform Building Code is a set of construction standards that has been adopted for many areas of the United States. Bricks meeting the Uniform Building Code standards are strong, durable, cannot be damaged by rain, and will withstand most stresses.

Most counties across the United States follow the Uniform Building Code requirements, and many lending institutions will not finance dwellings that do not comply with the code. Here is a summary of the Uniform Building Code requirements for adobe bricks.

1. The clay content of the soil used in producing adobe bricks must be greater than 25 percent and less than 45 percent.

2. Bricks are to be stabilized with emulsified asphalt and shall not absorb more than 2.5 percent water by weight (based on the dry weight of the adobe brick).

3. Bricks shall not have more than three shrinkage cracks. No shrinkage crack shall exceed 3 inches (7.6 cm) in length or be more than ¼ inch (.6 cm) wide.

4. The minimum compressive strength acceptable is 300 pounds (136.1 kg) per square inch (6.5 sq cm).

5. The average modulus of rupture for five bricks must be 50 pounds (22.7 kg) per square inch (6.5 sq cm), with no one individual brick testing out less than 35 pounds (15.8 kg) per square inch (6.5 sq cm).

(Write to the Building Officials Code Administrators International, 4051 W. Flossmoore Rd., Country Club Hills, IL 60478 / Website: www.bocai.org.)

TESTING THE STABILIZED BRICKS

Before you actually start making bricks you will need to determine the amount of emulsified asphalt needed for your particular soil. Local paving contractors should sell this product, or if not they can tell you who does. You will also find manufacturers listed on the Web. Search for emulsified asphalt. You can have this item delivered to your site or you can haul it yourself. To hold enough for your brick building you will need at least one 50-gallon drum. You can generally buy empty 50-gallon drums at surplus stores. (At times I have also found them at the local garbage dump.)

When buying emulsified asphalt, you should shop around for the best bargain. Prices vary, and you can often get a price break by buying 100 gallons or more.

Generally you will find ½ gallon (1.9 L) of emulsified asphalt per cubic foot (.03 cu m) of soil fairly satisfactory (that's ½ gallon for every 3½ bricks). Here is how to determine the amount of asphalt needed for your particular soil.

1. Construct a wooden box measuring 6 inches (15.2 cm) by 6 inches by 6 inches. This is ⅛ cubic foot (.004 cu m).

2. Fill the box with soil, measure 8 ounces (.2 L) of emulsified asphalt into a plastic measuring cup and add to soil.

3. Hand-shape this mixture into a small, 3 inch (7.6 cm) by 3 inch by 3 inch brick. Label and set aside.

4. Repeat this procedure with boxes full of soil mixed with 12 ounces (.4 L), 10 ounces (.3 L), 6 ounces (.2 L), and 4 ounces (.1 L) of emulsified asphalt. Label each brick as to the amount it contains.

5. Put these bricks on a cookie sheet and dry in the kitchen oven (200° to 400° F) for several hours. Before removing them all, break one open to make sure they have dried all the way through.

6. Immerse your test bricks in water for several hours. Bricks with enough emulsified asphalt will not soften along the edges. You want to use no more than the minimum amount of asphalt needed to waterproof your bricks, since too much will weaken them.

Following is a chart that will show you how much emulsified asphalt to use per brick.

**Amount of Emulsified Asphalt Needed per Brick
Utilizing a ⅛ Cubic Foot Test Box**

Measuring Cup oz of Asphalt per ⅛ cu ft Box	Gal per cu ft of Soil	Measuring Cup oz Needed per Brick
4	¼	9.1
6	⅜	13.7
8	½	18.2
10	⅝	22.9
12	¾	28.0
14	⅞	32.0

As soon as you have determined how much emulsified asphalt to use, go ahead and make a limited number of bricks. When your bricks are tested by a commercial lab, they will also be tested for water absorption, as required by the building department. However, any brick that passes your water test will absorb less than 2.5 percent moisture by weight. If you own a small scale you can also make your own moisture test.

It is possible to stabilize your bricks with portland cement in the ratio of 1 part cement to 12 parts soil. These bricks, while quite strong, are not waterproof and will not meet Uniform Building Code requirements.

Burnt adobe bricks are also used in some areas. These are simply kiln-fired adobe bricks. They are attractive and durable but are extremely absorbent and will flake severely in areas where frost is a problem.

Strength Tests

Following are two simple tests you can conduct at home to give you a general idea of just how strong your bricks are.

1. Once your bricks have been cured, try to break one by hand. Twist it with your hand, then put it down and stand on it. If your brick survives this test without breaking it is probably strong enough to meet minimum requirements.

2. You can also make a simple compression test using a sample adobe brick and two 2 x 4s nailed together as shown

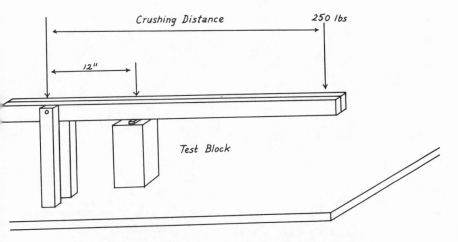

Crushing Distance   250 lbs

12"

Test Block

Figure 6. SIMPLE COMPRESSION TEST

in Figure 6. Start testing at the distance shown for 250 pounds (113.5 kg) per square inch (6.45 sq cm). If the brick doesn't break then move out and test for 300 pounds (136.1 kg) per square inch. If the brick passes this test it is probably acceptable.

	Compression Test	
	Crushing Distance for Bricks	
Area of	250 lb	300 lb
Test Block	per sq in	per sq in
4 sq in	3 ft 10 in	4 ft 7 in
6 sq in	5 ft 9 in	6 ft 11 in

As soon as you have produced a hundred or so bricks, have a commercial test made for compression and for modulus of rupture. I simply took two bricks to the lab and asked them to give me a written report. Then, when I finished my brickmaking, I selected three more bricks at random and had them tested. These written test reports were enough to satisfy the building department requirements.

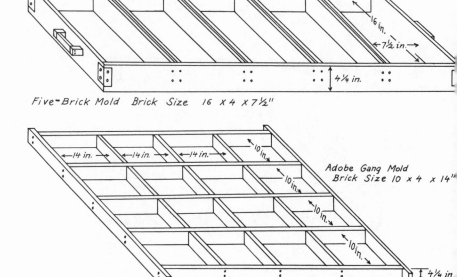

Figure 7. **ADOBE BRICK MOLDS**

MAKING YOUR ADOBE MOLDS

You will, of course, need some sort of mold to produce bricks. This can be a single mold or a multiple mold producing two or more bricks; the mold can be made of metal, wood, or anything else. In practice, I found a five-brick wooden mold worked best for me (Figure 7).

The standard size adobe brick used in post adobe construction and in 16-inch (40.6 cm) wide, double-brick, solid-wall construction is *4 inches by 7½ inches by 16 inches* (10 cm x 19 cm x 41 cm). The standard size brick in New Mexico and similar areas where the bricks are covered seems to be *4 inches by 10 inches by 14 inches* (10 cm x 25 cm x 36 cm).

Make the brick dimension the inside dimension of your

molds. The molds, however, should be made 4¼ to 4½ inches (11–12 cm) high, since the bricks generally slump when removed from the mold. My bricks actually ranged from 3½ to 5 inches (9–13 cm) in height—a variation that produced an interesting pattern in the finished walls.

Make all wooden molds from hardwood, Douglas Fir, or Southern Pine; these woods will withstand the wear and tear of brickmaking. The molds should be painted or shellacked inside to provide a slick surface. Rough surfaces make the bricks difficult to remove from the molds.

To build a five-brick mold cut two pieces 4¼ inches wide by 1 inch thick by 45 inches long (12 cm x 2.5 cm x 114 cm). Cut ten 4½ inch by 1 inch pieces 16 inches long (12 cm x 2.5 cm x 41 cm). Put the outer frame together with wood screws. Add two divider strips between each brick opening and make the bottom opening (for each brick) ¼ inch (.6 cm) wider than the top. This allows the brick to slip out easily. Add regular drawer handles at either end of your mold or make them out of scraps of wood. Also protect the four edges of your mold with sheet metal reinforcing (Figure 7).

Some adobe builders also make eight- to sixteen-brick molds out of 2 x 4s. Any mold, however, that makes more than eight bricks at a time requires two persons to lift off.

A clever innovation for making adobes is an 8 foot by 8 foot (2.4 m x 2.4 m) outer shell made of 2 x 4s. Pour the mud into the form and level it with a 2 x 4. After the mud sets for about two hours remove the outside 2 x 4s. Cut the adobes to size with a piano wire stretched across a 2 x 4 bow. This method is much faster than most others.

In addition to molds you can buy machine presses for casting bricks by hand. The CINVA Ram is a light, portable adobe press developed by the Inter American Housing and Planning Center (CINVA), Bogota, Columbia. CINVA Ram Inc., P.O. Box 59032, Orlando, FL 32859: Website: www.cinva-ram.com.

The bricks made from these presses are more uniform in size than hand-poured bricks. Since they are made under pressure they are also almost twice as strong as cast bricks. Generally, however, making bricks with a press is slower than casting with a form.

STARTING PRODUCTION

As soon as you have pretested your soil for clay content, established the amount of emulsified asphalt needed, and constructed your molds, you are ready to start producing bricks.

You now need a smooth, level surface on which to cast bricks, a mud mixer, emulsified asphalt, a bale of straw, a garden hose and nozzle attached to a water source (or a large barrel of water), a shovel, a pick for breaking hard ground, a rake, a trowel, and a large contractor's wheelbarrow.

To lay out my adobe bricks, I leveled a 30 foot by 40 foot (9 m x 12 m) area with a small tractor. I found this most satisfactory. Without leveling a large piece of land, however, you can cast bricks on a flat 8 foot by 3 foot (2.4 m x .9 m) casting surface made of ¾ inch (1.9 cm) plywood and 2 x 4s, or you can cast directly on large, level, ¾ inch pieces of plywood.

Next, to mix your adobe mud, I recommend that you purchase a contractor's plaster mixer. This is a large gas-powered mixer with turning blades used by contractors for mixing mortar and plaster for house construction. A cement mixer does not mix the adobe mud thoroughly enough. I feel strongly that a plaster mixer provides the best method for mixing bricks. After much searching I found a rental equipment operator willing to sell one of his used plaster mixers for $300. If you intend to buy a used one I would start with rental equipment operators, then call masonry contractors and firms specializing in used machinery.

When you are ready to start production, get everything—your pile of dirt, bale of straw (from a local feed and farm supply store), 50-gallon drum of emulsified asphalt, and plaster mixer—as close together as possible. In addition try to keep the distance between the mixer and the brick casting area as short as possible.

When you are ready to obtain soil from your site, you should try to blend the different layers of soil to make a uniform mix. One way is to combine the different layers in a pile with a shovel and then transfer this mixed soil with the shovel into your mud mixer. I don't care for this method because you must move the dirt twice. I found the best method is to create separate piles of each layer with a tractor, then shovel equal amounts from each layer into the mixer.

Figure 8. Loading a plaster mixer with "adobe" dirt. This is the easiest way of mixing adobe mud. Enough mud for 20 bricks can be loaded into this mixer at one time.

If you intend to mix the mud by hand, pile the soil in a 3 to 4 inch (8–10 cm) layer, add water, and "puddle" into a thick mud with a hoe. Mix thoroughly. When it is uniformly wet, add a 3 inch (8 cm) layer of straw and mix. Place in a wheelbarrow with a shovel, mix in the emulsified asphalt, and pour in the molds.

If you are using a plaster mixer, put 7 to 8 inches (18–20 cm) of water in the bottom, then add about 80 shovelfuls of soil. Add enough water to make a stiff mud. Beat the mud until the lumps are gone, then slowly add emulsified asphalt—about 2.5 gallons (9.5 L) per 20 bricks. Let this mix a couple of minutes (the asphalt will not darken the mud). Finally add the straw, about 1 part straw per 5 parts of soil. I simply cut the straw in 4 to 6 inch (10–15 cm) long pieces and placed it in a wooden box. When I had the box full I dumped it into the plaster mixer. When the straw is added the mixer slows down slightly.

The final mud mix should be thick enough to allow the brick to stand by itself once you take off the mold. With a few tries you will learn exactly how thick to make your own mix.

To pour the bricks I laid newspapers directly on the ground and placed four five-brick molds on top of the newspapers.

Do not pour the bricks directly on the ground since the wet mud will form a solid unit with the soil and spoil the brick.

Next, I poured the stiff mud into the wheelbarrow and dumped the mud from there into the molds. My contractor's wheelbarrow holds just enough mud to completely fill one five-brick mold. The plaster mixer itself holds enough to fill four five-brick molds. I then worked the mud up and down with a rake to fill out the sides and corners of the mold (Figure 10). When I was sure I had the mud into all the corners, I turned the rake over and leveled the brick surface even with the top of the molds. Many people use a trowel for this, but I find a trowel much too slow. As soon as I had the bricks leveled and fairly smooth, I slowly lifted off the molds. If you have made the mud stiff enough the bricks will stand by themselves with only slightly bulging sides. Do not allow the mud to set any length of time before removing the molds as this makes the bricks stick to the molds.

You must now clean your molds. I simply sprayed them with a hose, then scrubbed the molds down with a stiff brush. You can also completely immerse the molds in a tankful of water and clean them with a brush.

Then cover the newly made bricks with a few sheets of newspaper held in place at the corners with pieces of mud (Figure 12). In my early brickmaking days I did not shade the bricks; unfortunately, I often ended up with large cracks in each brick. I found that the newspapers slowed down evaporation and gave me almost perfect bricks every time. You will need to experiment with this. If your bricks dry in the open without cracking, fine. If not, utilize some sort of shade. You can make a more permanent shade than newspapers with 2 x 4s and plywood.

One other consideration: the rough surface left on top of the bricks by raking may in itself cause cracking. If you find this to be true with your own soil, smooth the bricks with a trowel instead of the back of a rake.

If a few bricks crack don't worry about it. You will need many part-bricks. I found, in practice, that I didn't have nearly enough part-bricks and frequently had to cut whole

Figure 9. Getting ready to pour bricks in a 5-brick mold. Bricks are poured on newspapers to prevent the bricks from sticking to the ground.

Figure 10. Raking a load of mud in a 5-brick mold. With some soils it is enough to rake the top smooth and let it dry. With other soils bricks handled this way will develop cracks. In cases of this type the bricks will have to be smoothed with a trowel.

Figure 11. Both tools and forms are washed after each batch of new adobe bricks is removed. The forms are tapered and shellacked so the bricks will slip out easily.

bricks to make the walls come out even between the posts.

As soon as your bricks have dried for three to four days, then stand them on end so they can dry on either side. After about six weeks, the moisture content will be down to about 4 percent. You can then stack them in groups. Simply place them on edge, three to four bricks high, against a center pillar. In my early brickmaking days I frequently stacked them seven to eight bricks high on wooden fruit pallets. This resulted in considerable breakage among the bottom bricks. Bricks stacked on edge store well for long periods of time.

To protect your bricks from the weather I recommend covering the piles with a piece of plywood, asphalt felt paper, or black plastic.

Also, as I mentioned earlier, it is important to build and store your bricks as near your building site as possible. You

Figure 12. Newspapers are placed on top of drying bricks to prevent cracking. It is necessary to experiment with your own bricks to see whether they dry best in the shade or in open sun.

Figure 13. Fresh-poured adobe bricks are covered with black plastic in preparation for a summer rain. Stabilized bricks like these can withstand almost any amount of water after they have dried.

must move approximately 2 tons (907 kg) of bricks for every 10 feet (3 m) of wall. To move this much weight any distance will consume a tremendous amount of time and energy. My own bricks, stored 100 to 200 feet (30–70 m) from the building site, required almost an hour's hauling time for every 10 feet of finished wall.

As you get into production you will soon learn how many bricks you can make a day. The first day I began, two of us produced exactly twenty-five bricks. I soon discovered that brickmaking is not an exact science. It always takes several tries to "work out the bugs." In the beginning I couldn't get the mud to fill out the sides of my bricks, many bricks had too many cracks, and others sagged so badly when I pulled off the molds that they couldn't possibly be used. You will be able to iron out difficulties like these after a few working days.

I found two people working together could produce about 225 bricks a day. Alone, I could make 125 to 150. Since I estimated 7,000 bricks were required for my 2,700 square foot (250 sq m) house—you need approximately 100 to 125 bricks for every 8 feet (2.4 m) of wall—I figured on thirty-three to thirty-five working days to make all the bricks. If you have only weekends for brick production, 5,000 bricks will require many weekends to produce.

Although making bricks is hard physical work, there is a great deal of satisfaction in knowing that you produced every last brick yourself, and in some ways I was almost sorry to see the brickmaking part come to an end.

4

Preparing and Building the Foundation

At this stage you need to level a pad for your house, dig the footing trenches, build foundation forms, pour the footings and foundation, and then either pour a slab or frame the floor. This chapter will take you through the steps required for each of these operations so you can do your own work easily and without hassle.

EXCAVATING THE SITE

Before you decide just how you are going to excavate a particular site, you should compare the cost of doing it yourself with the cost of hiring a contractor to do the work. First call local rental operators and ask their rental rates for a small crawler tractor with a blade. Then contact excavation or earth moving businesses to come out and give you an estimate. With these figures you should be able to make a decision.

When excavating, try to get the building site as level as possible. If you do not get it completely level at this stage, as I learned from sad experience, you will frequently have to put extra labor, materials, and money into building the foundation.

It is possible to determine the grades (levels) of your site at the building corners using a surveyor's level or a transit (available at most equipment rental yards), a hand-sight level (purchased from a drafting supply store), or a 2 foot or longer carpenter's level.

To make the actual grade determination, you will need two people, one to sight through or across the level and the other to hold an engineer's rod or stick. Simply set the level outside the building site at a spot slightly higher than any of the corners. A hand-sight level must be rested on a support.

Take a level measurement on the engineer's rod or stick at all four corners and note the distance from the level line-of-sight on the rod to the ground (Figure 14).

If the line-of-sight level at the first corner measures 4 feet (1.2 m) to the ground, the second corner 5 feet (1.5 m), and the third and fourth corners 3 feet (0.9 m), then you will need to cut the ground down almost 2 feet (0.6 m) in the vicinity of corners three and four.

Most builders do not cut a building site on a sloping lot to the lowest point, but cut the higher portion by digging, then filling the lower portion with excess dirt. This requires less work. In any case, the footings must rest on compact, undisturbed dirt and not on fill.

CORNER STAKING THE HOUSE

After you have leveled the building site, the next step is to set the stakes (called hubs) at all corners.

First stake one corner of your house. Then, using a metal tape, measure out one side of the house and drive the next stake. The measured distance should be between two nails driven in the tops of both stakes.

Now you can make a right angle at one corner and measure out to the next corner. These corners must be as square as you can make them. You can turn exact 90° corners with a transit. But most owner-builders use the 3-4-5 method—any triangle whose sides measure any multiple of 3,4,5 (6,8,10; 9,12,15 and similar measurements) has an exact 90° angle between the sides that measure 3 and 4 (Figure 15). This is by far the simplest method to lay out square corners on the ground since all you need is a tape measure.

Once you have the corner stakes set you should establish

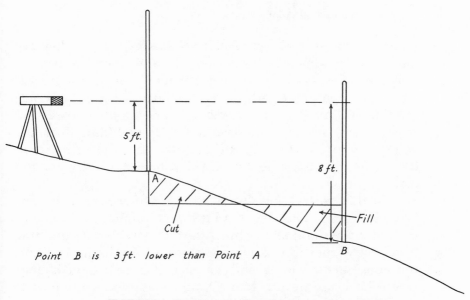

5 ft.

8 ft.

A

Cut

Fill

Point B is 3 ft. lower than Point A

B

Figure 14. **DETERMINING GRADE ELEVATIONS**

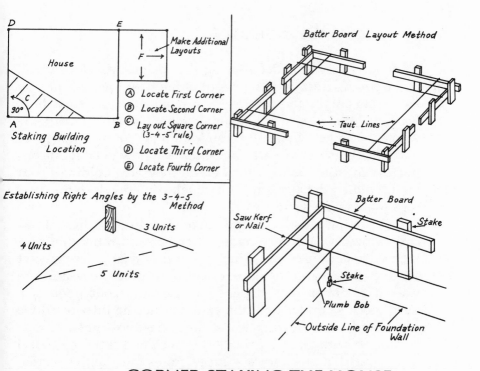

D   E

House

C
90°

A   B

Staking Building
Location

Make Additional
Layouts

F

Ⓐ Locate First Corner
Ⓑ Locate Second Corner
Ⓒ Lay out Square Corner
        (3-4-5 rule)
Ⓓ Locate Third Corner
Ⓔ Locate Fourth Corner

Establishing Right Angles by the 3-4-5
Method

3 Units

4 Units

5 Units

Batter Board Layout Method

Taut Lines

Batter Board

Saw Kerf
or Nail

Stake

Stake

Plumb Bob

Outside Line of Foundation
Wall

Figure 15. **CORNER STAKING THE HOUSE**

batter boards so you can reset your stakes anytime they are lost digging trenches. Batter boards are simply a pair of stakes with a board nailed across them. To mark the board, stretch a nylon line tightly across the boards along the building line and mark with a saw cut where the line crosses the boards. Now anytime you need to find the building lines just stretch the nylon lines tightly over the saw marks between the batter boards. The lines will intersect exactly on the corners.

At this point I am always so eager to see what the finished house will look like that I lay it out on the site and mark the outer walls and all the inner partitions with marking lime (available at most building supply stores). In doing so, I find the house always looks smaller on the ground than it does when the walls are up. Many times when you see the bedrooms and other rooms laid out this way you will want to enlarge them. Don't; once the walls are up these rooms will feel much larger than they do now.

DIGGING THE FOOTINGS

All footings must be deep enough in the ground so they will be below the frost line (the depth of the frost line depends on your climate). If the footings are not below the frost line, water or moisture may get under them, freeze, and lift the whole building. Generally you can find out how deep to make footings in your area by observing how deep local contractors dig the footings for houses they are building. Your local building department can also tell you how deep the footings must be for your area.

A footing must be in the range of 12 to 18 inches (30–46 cm) below the ground (grade). It must be a minimum of 8 inches (20 cm) thick and 4 inches (10 cm) to 50 percent wider on each side than the adobe bricks you intend to use in the wall. The dimensions depend on the local code. You will need footings under both the exterior and the interior adobe walls (and other bearing walls), and these footings must be reinforced with two pieces of #4 ½ inch (1.3 cm) rebar (steel bars, available at building supply stores and lumber yards) that extend through the entire footing.

The fireplace foundation must also be a concrete slab

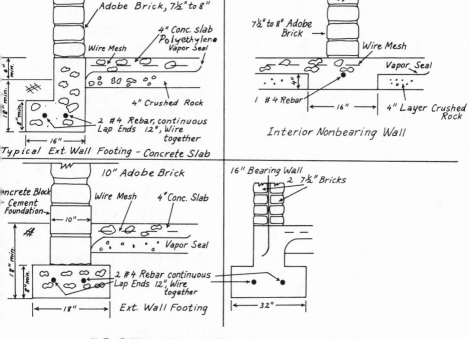

Figure 16. FOOTINGS—FOUNDATIONS—SLABS
(for different types of adobe construction)

12 inches (30 cm) thick, 4 inches (10 cm) larger than the basic fireplace structure, and reinforced with ½ inch rebar spaced 12 inches (30 cm) apart. (See Chapter 9 for more about planning and building fireplaces.)

You can dig the footing trenches by hand, rent a trencher, or hire a contractor to dig them for you. In my own case I broke up the hard-packed earth with a Rototiller, then dug out the loose dirt by hand.

Once you complete the footing trenches, lay two pieces of ½ inch (1.2 cm) rebar about 10 inches (20 cm) apart in the trenches. Support each piece of rebar 4 inches (10 cm) above the bottom of the trench by driving shorter pieces of rebar into the trench bottom and tying the longer rebar to it with wire, or by using broken pieces of concrete block. Overlap the rebar lengths a minimum of 12 inches and tie tightly with wire (available from the supplier where you bought the rebar).

You can now estimate the amount of concrete needed for the footings by converting the width and depth of your footings to feet, then multiplying the width and depth by the total length of your footings. This gives you the number of cubic feet of concrete needed. When ordering from a ready-mix firm, however, you will need to tell them how much you need in cubic yards, so divide the total number of cubic feet by 27.

For example, let's say your footings are 8 inches (20 cm) thick, 18 inches (46 cm) wide, and 110 feet (33.5 m) long:

$$8 \text{ in} = .66 \text{ ft}$$
$$18 \text{ in} = 1.5 \text{ ft}$$
$$.66 \text{ ft} \times 1.5 \text{ ft} \times 110 \text{ ft} = 108.9 \text{ cu ft}$$
$$108.9 \div 27 = 3.8 \text{ cu yd } (2.8 \text{ cu m})$$

If you plan to mix the concrete yourself, one bag equals 1 cu ft. Here is the formula to use for mixing concrete for both the footings and the slab.

	Parts Cement	Parts Sand	Parts Gravel	Gallons of Water per Sack
Footings	1	3	5	7½
Slab	1	2	3	6

If you intend to use a ready-mix concrete, make sure that you can drive the truck around the entire house. The concrete mix can be placed up to 20 feet from the truck with the chute that is a part of the truck equipment. Beyond that distance you will have to haul the concrete in a wheelbarrow or pump it.

Once you pour the foundation footing, you have several choices. If you intend to construct a wood floor, you will now build a foundation wall out of hollow concrete blocks that you fill with cement, or you will build forms and pour a concrete foundation wall. Or, and this is my choice, you can build your house on a concrete slab.

If the foundation wall (stem) is to be made out of concrete blocks, the top of the footings must be made level. To

Figure 17. Constructing the foundation for an adobe house. The footings are poured in place first, then the concrete slab is poured on top of them.

do this, drive grade stakes at the edge of the footing trench: first drive one stake to within 8 inches (20 cm) above the bottom of the trench, then with a carpenter's level set the other stakes. Figure 17 shows these stakes set up.

You can also level the top of the forms for a foundation wall by utilizing rebar driven into the bottom of the footing ditch. Simply level the tops with a transit or surveyor's level as we did with the building site (some builders also use a carpenter's level for this operation). You can now pour the concrete for both the footing and the foundation wall around the rebar.

If you intend to pour a concrete slab you can make the slab and the footings all one and pour at the same time. If local code permits, this is the easiest way. After you have dug the footing trenches, drive wooden stakes at the edge of the footing to within 6 inches (15 cm) above the ground (grade); then, using a transit or surveyor's level, place grade stakes about 4 feet (1.4 m) apart all the way around the outside.

When the stakes are level you can nail a 2 x 6 to them and brace the 2 x 6. This will give you a form in which to pour the slab. Where the code insists that the footing extend beyond the wall on both sides, you will have to pour the footing first, then build forms and pour the slab.

POURING THE CONCRETE SLAB

After the footing trenches have been dug and the forms built for the slab, you will need to put down 4 inches (10 cm) of gravel or crushed stone and a moisture barrier of heavy polyethylene and construction wire mesh (see Figure 16, page 53). The polyethylene moisture barrier and construction wire can be purchased from most lumber yards.

It is possible for anyone to pour his or her own concrete. However, when you are trying to work a large slab you may run into difficulties, as it begins to dry or to "set up." While I did most of the work on my own slab, I hired a skilled finisher to help with the actual pouring. (I found this person by asking the concrete-truck driver to recommend someone.)

After pouring the concrete you will need to rough-level it with a screed—a straight 2 x 4 moved across the tops of the forms to scrape away excess concrete that is higher than the form. Level repeatedly as you fill the form until you reach the end of the slab. If your slab is too wide to reach across with your screed, place temporary screed bars (2 x 4s) on center stakes and then run the screed from the top of the form to the top of the screed bars (Figure 18).

As you finish particular areas, remove the screed bars and fill the holes left with a shovel. Once the form is filled and screeded reasonably smooth, use a jitterbug or hand tamper (Figure 18) over the entire surface to submerge the protruding aggregate.

When this is finished you must trowel the surface with a trowel on a long handle (called a bull float). The concrete is then allowed to dry (set up) to the point where a board will not sink.

It can now be troweled by hand or with a gasoline-powered mechanical trowel (used for large slabs) available from any local equipment rental firm. If you want a really smooth slab, trowel the whole slab at least twice.

The concrete slab will set up in a few hours, but it

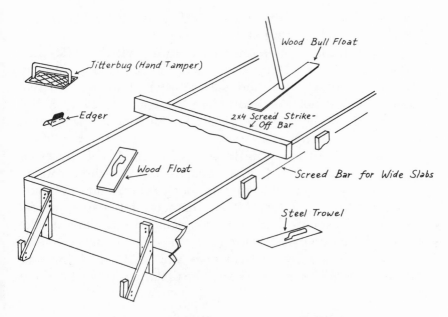

Figure 18. **CEMENT SLAB TOOLS**

usually takes all day to finish any large slab. Once the slab has been poured and finished you should prevent it from drying too rapidly by sprinkling it with a hose when it starts to dry out. This should be continued for a day or two to insure a good surface.

FRAMING THE FLOOR

Some adobe builders prefer a wooden floor to a concrete slab. With a wooden floor, piers and posts rest on concrete footings and, along with the foundation walls, support the wooden beams (girders), joists, and flooring (Figure 19).

The wooden girders placed across the foundation can be solid or made of two pieces of 2 inch (5 cm) lumber nailed together. Joists (the parallel pieces of lumber that hold up the floor) usually run from one side of the foundation to the other and are supported by both the girders and the foundation.

The joists are nailed to pieces of lumber (headers) at either end or there are small pieces of lumber (blocking) nailed between the joists at the ends. Blocking should also be placed between the joists at midspan.

Many building departments require that the joists rest on a piece of treated lumber (a mud sill) rather than directly on the concrete. This mud sill is fastened to the concrete foundation by bolts embedded in the concrete every 8 feet (2.4 m). The bolts must be placed in the concrete when you pour the foundation wall.

Posts are usually constructed of short 4 x 4 pieces of lumber spaced 5 feet (1.5 m) apart. Concrete piers can be purchased ready-made from a lumber yard or made by pouring concrete into 1 foot (.3 m) diameter felt paper molds. Footings are square and have the same dimensions as the width of the outer wall footing.

The following table will give you an idea of the size lumber needed for the joists and the distance apart (called the

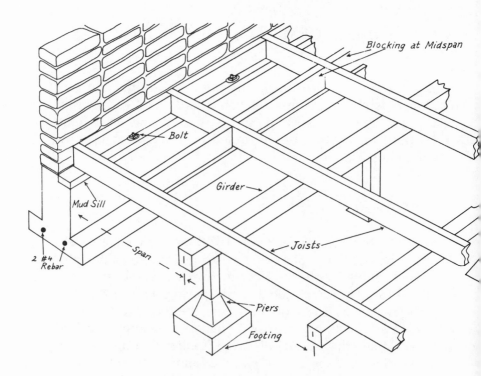

Figure 19. WOOD FLOOR FRAMING
FOUNDATION

allowable span) you can space the girders. Many building departments will give you a span table similar to this when you pick up your building permit.

After you complete your foundations, the next step—putting up the walls—always seems to go fairly rapidly.

Allowable Spans for Floor Joists
(40 lbs per sq ft live load)

Joist size (in)	Spacing (in)	Douglas Fir Joists		
		Grade 3	Grade 2	Grade 1
2 x 6	12	9' 2"	10' 11"	11' 2"
	16	7' 9"	9' 11"	10' 2"
	24		8' 6"	8' 10"
2 x 8	12	12' 1"	14' 5"	14' 8"
	16	10' 7"	12' 1"	13' 4"
	24		11' 3"	11' 8"
2 x 10	12	15' 5"	18' 5"	18' 9"
	16	13' 6"	16' 9"	17' 0"
	24		14' 4"	14' 11"
2 x 12	12	18' 9"	22' 5"	22' 10"
	16	15' 10"	20' 4"	20' 9"
	24		17' 5"	18' 1"

5
Putting Up Adobe Walls

There are several systems utilized today in constructing adobe walls. Which system you use depends primarily on whether or not you are building in earthquake country. In New Mexico, for instance, the code allows the builder to lay bricks into a self-supporting wall without reinforcement. In California, where you must consider earthquakes, you are required to use either steel reinforcing rods or a wooden post-frame support. Each of these systems will be explained later in this chapter.

GETTING YOUR EQUIPMENT TOGETHER

No matter where you build, the equipment needed to lay bricks is about the same. My own list includes the following: wheelbarrow, mason's trowel, joint tool, wire brush, shovel, hone, brick splitter or wide chisel, a long level (or mason's level), nylon cord, gloves, nails, and a story pole.

MIXING MORTAR

The best formula for mortar that is to be used in laying up exposed adobe bricks is to use the same type of mortar as the bricks are made of: 1 part cement to 2½ parts sand. This mortar is waterproofed by adding 1½ gallons (5.7 L) of emulsified asphalt to each sack of cement.

In New Mexico, where the adobe bricks are covered with plaster, most builders utilize adobe mud mortar, which is adobe dirt that is first screened to remove rocks, then mixed with water to form a stiff paste.

The rule is: If the bricks are exposed, use a waterproof cement or asphalt mortar; if the building department allows and your walls are to be plastered, use adobe mud as mortar.

You can either mix adobe mud in a cement mixer, or mix it directly in a contractor's wheelbarrow with a hoe, making only a small amount of mortar at a time.

LAYING ADOBE BRICKS PROPERLY

You will find it useful to estimate roughly the number of bricks needed in a wall section before you start to lay up the wall itself. I find that I am able to work much faster if I have the approximate number of bricks as near as possible to the section I am going to work. A simple guideline is to count on 150 to 155 16-inch (40 cm) bricks and 160 to 165 14-inch (37 cm) bricks for every 10 feet (3.1 m) of wall.

Unless your window widths are well over 4 feet (1.2 m), do not make any allowance in your calculations for windows or doors. This will give you some overallowance for breakage and the loss that always occurs when you have to split bricks.

To start laying your bricks, wet the top of the foundation and place some mortar on it, spreading the mortar with a trowel to a ¾ inch (2 cm) thickness. Next, set the two end bricks in the wall or wall section.

Place string guides along the wall by driving two nails in each end brick as shown in Figure 20. Tie a nylon cord to the nails in the other corner brick. This will allow you to keep the top of each course level; however, you must take considerable care with the corners to insure they are straight vertically. Check frequently with your level.

You will also find a story pole useful in keeping each course of bricks at the proper height. A story pole is a pole on which you have marked off the top of each brick course to the top of the wall.

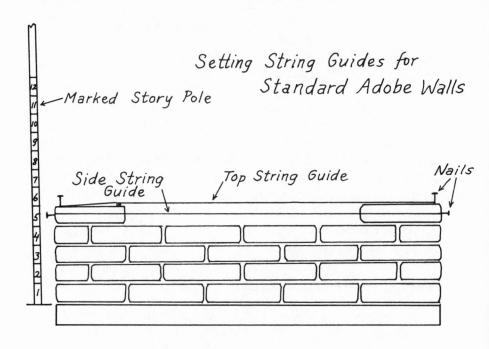

Setting String Guides for Standard Adobe Walls

Marked Story Pole

Side String Guide

Top String Guide

Nails

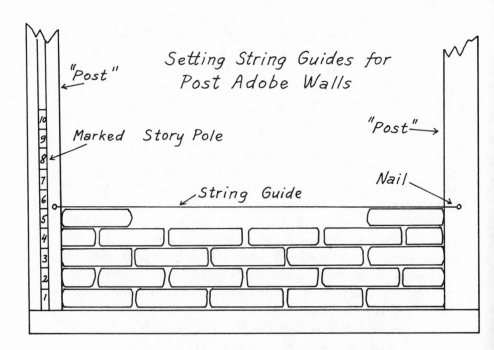

Setting String Guides for Post Adobe Walls

"Post"

Marked Story Pole

"Post"

String Guide

Nail

Figure 20. **SETTING STRING GUIDES**

Adobes average about 4 inches (10 cm) thick. The recommended joint thickness is ¾ inch (2 cm). If you allow ¾ inch for the first joint, the top of the first brick should then be marked on your story pole at 4¾ inches (12 cm), the top of the next brick at 9½ inches (24 cm), and so on, until you reach the desired wall height minus the bond beam (see section on bond beams, page 65).

Since adobe is not a perfect material, the height of the bricks will vary somewhat. I found that mine ranged from 3½ to 5 inches (9–13 cm). If you simply keep the tops of each row level as you put your bricks up, however, the rows will look quite uniform.

Now continue laying your adobes from one corner to the other end. When you start the next row, overlap your adobe bricks by 50 percent (Figure 20). Fill the vertical joints with mortar after you complete each course. If your bricks are to be plastered over do not worry about the appearance. However, if they are to be exposed, take care to make the tops of each row as straight as possible.

To give the finished bricks a neat, tailored appearance, rake the joint back about half an inch with a raking tool after the mortar has hardened to the point where it is still workable. Now take a steel brush and clean the mortar off the bricks themselves.

If you like a "weeping mortar" appearance, do not rake the mortar joints back, but clean the mortar from the bricks before it dries.

ALLOWING FOR DOORS AND WINDOWS

Wherever you intend to place doors and windows in your wall you must build what is called a rough buck. This is a rough lumber frame that provides a rectangular opening to receive a door or window. The rough buck frame is usually made of 2 x 8 or 2 x 10 lumber braced and supported as shown in Figures 21 and 22.

To tie the wooden frames to the adobes, 1 inch by 4 inch by 18 inch wooden nailers are laid between the bricks in the mortar. The rough frame is then nailed to these nailers. To

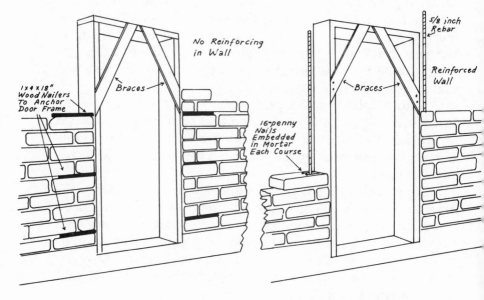

Figure 21. **ROUGH BUCKS FOR DOORS**

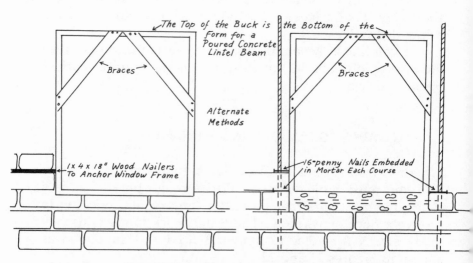

Figure 22. **ROUGH BUCKS FOR WINDOWS**

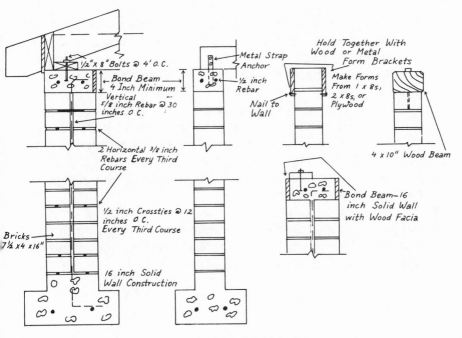

Figure 23. **BOND BEAMS**

allow for finishing, the rough frame should be made about 3 inches (8 cm) wider and longer than the door or window you intend to install.

BOND BEAMS AND LINTELS

Bond Beams

The tops of all masonry walls (except post adobe) are tied together with a concrete or wood bond beam (Figure 23). This is because all walls tend t o spread and crack unless tied together at the top. The bond beam is usually concrete, a minimum of 4 inches (10 cm) thick, and reinforced with one or more steel reinforcing rods (½ inch rebar).

Build your forms for the bond beams from 1 x 8 or 2 x 8 lumber. Nail the bottom of the lumber to the wall and tie the tops together with metal brackets or pieces of 1 to 2 inch

(2.5–5 cm) lumber nailed across the top of the forms. The rebar can be supported on pieces of wire nailed between the two sides of the forms or on vertical rebar. At this point you will also need to place in the bond beam some sort of anchoring method to be used in securing the roof (see Chapter 10, page 127).

You can mix your own concrete for these bond beams at a ratio of 1 part cement to 3 parts gravel to 2 parts sand, or you can buy ready-mix concrete. I have seen builders mix the concrete for the bond beam in a wheelbarrow, but if you plan to mix it yourself you will save a tremendous amount of work by renting a small cement mixer.

You may also use a heavy wooden bond beam on top of the walls. This wooden bond beam should be a minimum of 4 inches (10 cm) thick, and the ends and corners should be fastened together securely.

Lintels

Lintels are simply bridges over openings in the walls where windows and doors will be. These lintels should be 12 inches (30 cm) thick over openings up to 8 feet (2.4 m) long, and 18 inches (46 cm) over openings longer than 8 feet. Extend the lintel 6 to 9 inches (15–22 cm) beyond all wall openings.

To make lintel forms use 2 x 8s or 1 x 8s nailed into the bricks. The tops of all window and door rough bucks (the wooden window and door frames) are the bottoms of the lintel forms (Figure 24). Since lintels are essentially a thickening of the bond beam over doors and windows it is probably easier to make all forms together and pour as one piece.

You may also use wooden lintels over all window and door openings. These must extend 12 to 18 inches (31–46 cm) beyond any opening. Steel lintels may also be used.

STEEL REINFORCING

In earthquake areas, one way of meeting the code is to utilize both horizontal and vertical steel reinforcing rods (rebar) in the walls.

Vertical rebar is placed on 2 to 4 foot (.6–1.2 m) centers

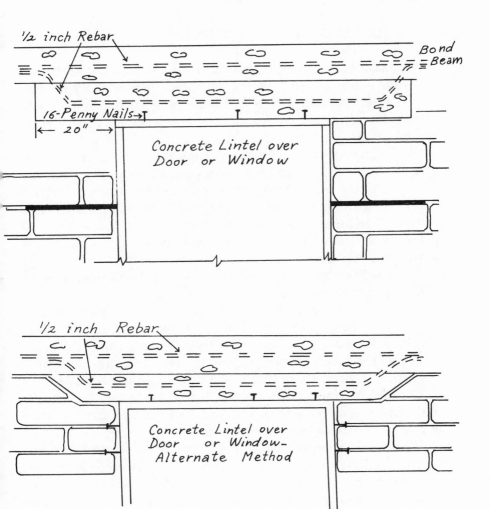

Figure 24. **CONCRETE LINTELS**

and tied to the reinforcing steel in the footings. If you are building a single-brick-width adobe wall, split the adobes to allow for the rebar or drill holes in the brick. If you are building a double-brick adobe wall, the vertical rebar will run between the bricks. Tie a double wall together with pieces of rebar 12 inches (31 cm) on center with every other course.

With both single- and double-brick walls you must place horizontal rebar every third course as shown in Figure 23.

POST ADOBE CONSTRUCTION

Post adobe construction has been utilized in California for many years, producing some attractive contemporary homes.

After the foundation has been poured, the first step in building a post adobe house is to construct a wooden frame wall utilizing posts and a "beam" at the top. This post and beam construction then supports the roof, which is built directly on it. (For more about roofs, see Chapter 10.) Posts are placed in the post adobe frame at all corners, every 8 feet (2.4 m) along the wall, and on either side of all windows and doors (see Figure 26). Bricks are laid between the posts to fill the open space. The bricks do not, however, support any weight other than their own.

For the posts you can use 6 x 6s, 8 x 8s, railroad ties, or any type of built-up post.

For my own adobe I utilized a rough, 4 inch (10 cm) redwood inner post with 2 x 6s nailed to either side. This gave me a post that was 7½ inches (19 cm) wide, the same size as the bricks. When the bricks were laid into the wall a ¾ inch (1.9 cm) space that was left between the edge of the 2 x 6s and the interior post was filled with mortar. This closed the opening between the post and the bricks so that the wind couldn't come through the cracks.

Building departments unfamiliar with post adobe construction often insist that the frame be engineered. However, since the post adobe frame is standard for this type of construction and has been in use for many years, an engineered frame is really unnecessary. Unfortunately you will have to comply with whatever the building department in your area requires.

Placing the Post Holders

A number of methods are used to keep the posts in place, including ½ inch (1.3 cm) anchor pins set in concrete, and large bolts. The best method is to use standard post holders (available at building supply stores). These are metal holders with prongs that extend into the concrete. The post is inserted in the post holder and nailed into place.

Figure 25. Four-by-four-inch posts in place on the concrete foundation. After a header beam is added, the bricks are simply filled in between the posts. This method provides an extremely strong frame for a post adobe house.

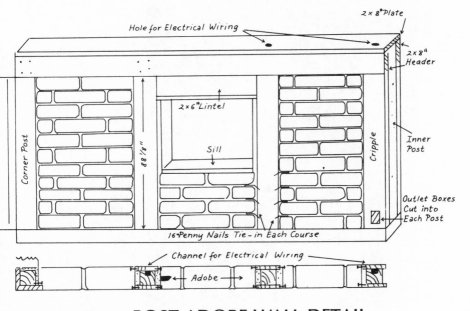

Figure 26. **POST ADOBE WALL DETAIL**

Figure 27. Post holders in place on a concrete slab foundation. These posts must be set in a straight line and spaced at the proper intervals while the concrete is still wet.

Figure 28. Placing posts for a post adobe house in post holders. The post holders embedded in concrete are nailed directly to the posts.

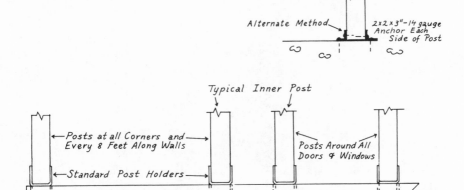

Figure 29. **POST ANCHORING METHODS**

Post holders must be set in place while the concrete is wet. Along the walls you can simply mark the foundation forms and insert the post holders after you pour the concrete. As mentioned, posts go at all corners, a minimum of 8 feet (2.4 m) apart along the walls, and around all doors and windows (Figure 29).

Around doors and windows you must leave approximately 2½ inches (6 cm) at each post for framing. If the window is to be 4 feet (1.2 m) wide, the distance between the two posts should be 4 feet, 5 inches (1.3 m).

Post holders for interior walls must be set in a straight line or you will create a bulge in the wall. To insure a straight line, place strings (line) along the middle of the proposed wall from one side of the foundation to the other. With chalk, mark the line where the post holders go and take the line off one side. When the concrete is poured, put the line back and insert the post holders in the proper position.

Headers and Top Plates

The wooden beam at the top of the post adobe wall can be made of solid 6 x 6s, or 8 x 8s if you desire. Most modern post

Figure 30. (*a*) Nailing the top plates and header beams in place. Note the 2 x 6 cripples below this.

(*b*) Adobe bricks are then added as a filler wall; each layer is kept straight with a string line. A two-inch layer of mortar is added above the top row of bricks after the bricks reach the header beam.

adobe construction utilizes a hollow "beam" consisting of two 2 x 8 top plates and 2 x 8 pieces (header beams) on either side.

The easiest way to install these "beams" is to utilize a 4 x 4 inner post with 2 x 6 pieces (cripples) 88½ inches (225 cm) long on either side to hold the 2 x 8 header beams. These 2 x 8 header beams are placed on top of the cripples and nailed into place using four 16-penny galvanized nails at each post. After the header beams are nailed into place, then nail two 2 x 8 plates on top of these to form a "hollow beam."

Rough Framing the Doors and Windows

Post adobe construction requires a post on either side of all doors and windows. Windows are rough framed by a header at the top, a rough sill at the bottom, and a trimmer on either side the same width as the post (Figure 31). Doors are framed by a header and two trimmers on either side.

Because you will need a sash around windows and doors add an extra 2½ inches (6.3 cm) to all window and door heights and widths.

Figure 31. Wall of a post adobe house. Note posts around all doors and windows. The adobes in this house do not contribute to the structural support. The posts carry the entire weight of the roof.

Interior Walls

Interior walls can be built of adobe bricks or by standard wood frame construction.

If you are not building a post adobe frame house, tie the interior walls to the exterior walls by overlapping the bricks exactly as you would for a corner wall. You might also have to pour a bond beam for these interior walls that is tied to the bond beam of the exterior walls.

If you are building a post adobe frame house, install a post at the junction of an interior adobe wall with an exterior adobe wall and build that wall directly into the post.

You will need to plan for anchoring kitchen cabinets to the interior wall. See Chapter 11, page 150, for details.

Wood Frame Construction   Wood frame interior walls are often used in adobe houses because they are easier to build than adobe walls. They also make excellent plumbing walls, since it is difficult to lay adobe bricks around pipes.

Construct wood frame walls of 2 x 4s as shown in Figure 32. When you are building a plumbing wall and the pipes are not quite in line, construct the wall of 2 x 6s instead of 2 x 4s.

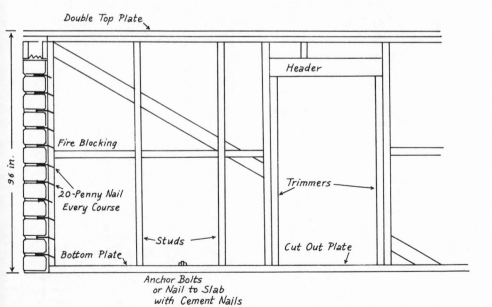

Figure 32. **INTERIOR STUD WALLS**

To lay out the wall plate, take the bottom and top 2 x 4s (called plates) and cut them the exact length of the wall you intend to build. Then nail the plates together as shown. If the wall is longer than the 2 x 4s you are using, add 2 x 4s to reach the desired length.

Now take a tape measure and starting at one end make a mark with a pencil every 16 inches (41 cm) on the edge of the two plates. This marks the center of the wall studs (vertical 2 x 4s). Two 2 x 4 trimmers also go around each door and window as shown.

Some builders like to mark the edge of each stud instead of the center. Since the standard width of most 2 x 4s is 1½ inches (3.8 cm), the first edge would fall 15¼ inches (39.4 cm) from the corner, the second 31¼ inches (80 cm), and so forth.

After you have marked the plates, taken them apart, cut the 2 x 4s to size, and nail the wall plate together according to your plan. As noted, headers (supporting pieces) go over each door and window. When you are finished, stand the wall plate up, place it into the proper position, and nail it to the floor with cement nails.

You can tie this wall into an adobe wall by placing nailers between the adobe blocks as you build the wall (much as we did for the rough bucks). Or you can build the stud wall first, joining the two walls with 20-penny nails by embedding the heads of the 20-penny nails in the mortar of the joints, as shown in Figure 32.

6
Installing the Plumbing System

There is absolutely no reason why you can't install your own plumbing system. Every year hundreds of thousands of owner-builders do their own plumbing and seem to have very little trouble.

Generally the system in an adobe house divides neatly into two separate areas: the drainage system, installed in an early stage of building, and the water supply system, put in after the walls are up.

THE DRAINAGE SYSTEM

If you are building on a concrete slab, as many adobe builders do, you will need to construct the drainage system after you build the forms but before you pour the slab.

With the drainage system, the water that runs out of the fixtures (tub, shower, lavatory, sink, washing machine, toilet) must be carried away by the drain. Gases created by decomposition within the system must be dispelled outside through vents or stacks (vertical pipes) that extend through the roof.

If a toilet empties into a stack, the stack is called the main soil stack. Other stacks are called secondary soil stacks. In a one-story house with more than one toilet, the last stack before the drain leaves the house is called the main stack.

Each fixture is joined to its stack by a branch drain that must slope downward toward the stack. Fixtures may be vented into the stack through their waste pipes (called wet venting) if they are close enough to the stack. Under the National Plumbing Code a tub or shower may be wet vented if it is within 3½ feet (1.1 m) from the trap outlet to the soil stack. A lavatory may be wet vented if its trap outlet is within 2½ feet (.8 m) of the stack.

If the fixtures are farther than this from the stack, they need separate pipes running from the fixture up through the roof, or they need to be connected to a soil stack by a horizontal pipe that is higher off the floor than the highest fixture drain connection (Figure 33). This is called a revent. Horizontal revent pipes are pitched slightly upward from the fixture to allow the condensation to drain back toward the fixture.

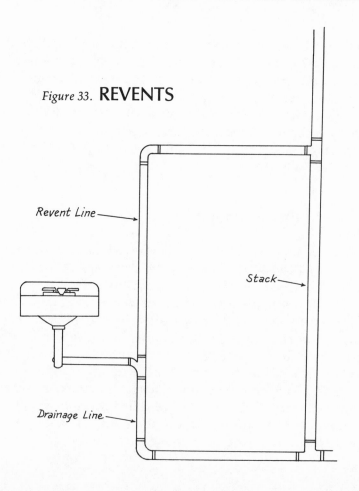

Figure 33. REVENTS

Revent Line

Stack

Drainage Line

Laying Out a Drain Plan

You should start your drain plan when you start to plan the house. You will save on materials if you place the fixtures back-to-back in two different bathrooms, or the bathroom and kitchen. That way the fixtures in both rooms can use the same main lines.

You will also save pipe and labor if you keep the rooms with the fixtures as near each other as possible. In my own house, I planned two separate wings. One wing contained the kitchen, two bathrooms, and a laundry room. Fifty feet away across the house I planned the master bedroom with a large bath. This plan cost at least $500–$600 more than it would have if I had kept all the bathrooms close to each other.

In laying out your drain plan use an extra copy of your floor plan and mark the drain plan on it in pencil. Locate the main stack first and mark it. This is the last stack before the drain leaves the house. You can connect two toilets to the main stack if the bathrooms are back to back.

Now connect (on paper) the nearby fixtures, such as the shower and sink, to the main stack. You can also connect a washing machine drain into a main stack if your utility room and bathroom are back to back.

Next, make a note of any sinks over 2½ feet (.8 m) from the main stack and showers or tubs over 3½ feet (1.1 m) from the main stack. These must be connected to the main stack with a horizontal pipe raised off the floor (revented).

Finally, draw in the drain pipe that connects all the fixtures. Your object is to run the drain in a straight line and connect the soil stack with the least amount of pipe. Take a straightedge and pencil in a few possibilities. From these select the plan that looks best to you.

After you locate the drain pipe, mark the cleanouts. You will need one at each end of the main drain and at the ends of all branch lines. If you are building on a concrete slab, locate them outside the foundation, whenever possible. Otherwise place them at the bottom of the soil stack as shown in Figure 34, on the next page.

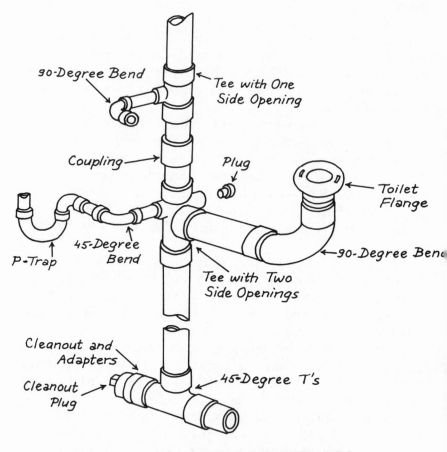

Figure 34. **PLASTIC PIPE FITTINGS**

How to Select the Right Fittings

Plastic drain pipe is easiest to use. It is lightweight and can be assembled quickly using a small saw and plastic cement. This pipe is available in 1½ inch (3.8 cm), 2 inch (5 cm), and 3 inch (7.6 cm) sizes in 10 foot (3.1 m) lengths.

Generally the building drain and the main stack are of 3 inch plastic pipe. The secondary soil stacks should be the size of the largest branch drain that connects to them. The pipe sizes from the branch drains and revent lines are determined by the type of fixture.

Type of Fixture	All Drains and Revent Lines
Lavatory	1½"
Tub or Shower	1½"
Toilet	3"
Sink	1½–2"
Garbage Disposal	1½–2"
Dishwasher	1½–2"
Clothes Washer	1½–2"

You now have choices to make among the following accessory fixtures (Figure 34).

couplings (to join pipes)
plugs
tees (with one or two
    openings)
toilet bend
toilet flange

P-traps
cleanouts and adapters
cleanout plugs
3 and 4 inch (7.6 and 10.2 cm)
    spigot adapters
45° Ts

The easiest way to decide what you need is to make a rough sketch around each stack and pencil in the needed accessories. From this make an inventory list as shown in Figure 34.

Preparing the Drainage Trenches

When you are ready to put the drainage system together, lay out your building drain line and secondary drain lines on the ground using nylon cord. Mark the foundation where the drain is to go through or under it. Now dig a trench 2 feet (.6 m) wide, with this cord as its center, and deep enough so the bottom will never be more than 1 foot (.3 m) below the surface of the finished slab. Now grade the trench 1¼ inch (.7 cm) per 5 feet (1.5 m), starting at the far end and working toward the point where the drain will go out through the foundation. It is important that the pitch of the pipe be as close to 1¼ inch per 5 feet as you can make it. If you make the pitch less than this the solids won't be washed along with the water; if you make it more, the solids will form an obstruction in the pipe.

Grade all secondary branch drains to the same pitch. After you complete the trench inside the foundation, extend it at least 5 feet outside the foundation.

How to Cut and Fit Plastic Pipe

Cutting and fitting plastic pipe is extremely simple. I personally always have trouble gluing and fitting anything, but plastic pipe is so easy I usually do it right the first time.

To cut plastic pipe, use a hacksaw, a handsaw, or a power saw, but never use a rotary pipe cutter. The saw blade should be fairly fine-toothed (9–14 teeth per inch with little set). To be sure the cuts are square you can build a jig out of a block of wood to hold the saw and pipe. If you use a vise, wrap the pipe in cloth to prevent damaging the pipe surface.

To make connections, clean both the inside of the fitting and the surface of the pipe to be inserted in the fitting. Apply solvent to both surfaces and press the pipe and fitting firmly together. Turn the pipe one-quarter turn to distribute the solvent evenly. Next hold the pieces together for about fifteen seconds. Clean off any excess solvent with a rag.

Installing the Drainage System

You now need to locate the toilet, shower, and bathtubs, plus the location of the drain pipes in the plumbing wall for the sinks and other fixtures.

You need 24 inches (70 cm) of space between the front of the toilet and the finished wall, and 15 inches (31 cm) of space between the toilet and the finished wall or other fixtures.

Place the toilet bend in position and fasten in place by driving a piece of rebar into the ground, securing the pipe to the rebar with wire. Now cement the toilet floor flange to the toilet bend, making sure the floor flange is set exactly at finished floor height. This is important because you can easily cover it over when you pour cement, or you can misjudge and end up by having toilet flange be 2 to 3 inches (5–7.6 cm) above the finished floor.

Figure 35. ABS pipe is easy for a beginner to put together. The entire drain system for this 2,700 sq ft house was laid out within a few hours.

If you are installing the toilet bend and flange through a wooden floor, simply hold the pipe and flange in place by nailing a brace underneath the toilet bend as shown.

You will find it easier not to install the drain for the shower or tub until after you have poured the slab. Simply construct a 1 foot (.3 m) wide wooden box in the approximate position of the drain. Fill the box with sand to within 1 to 2 inches (2.5–5 cm) of the top of the floor. When you are ready to install the bathtub or shower, you can break through the floor and install the trap and floor flange. The 1 foot (.3 m) box will allow you to adjust the trap and floor flange to the shower drain.

Now extend the pipes for all other fixtures 12 to 18 inches (31–46 cm) above the finished slab. Fasten them in place with wire and rebar. Make sure these pipes are in an absolutely straight line or you will have trouble later fitting them inside a 2 x 4 plumbing wall. Wherever any pipe will extend through the concrete, wrap that pipe with insulation.

Now pour the slab and continue with your building. The additional work will be completed later.

If you are installing the sewage system underneath a floor in a crawl space (instead of under a concrete slab) you will hang the pipe from hangers and brackets.

After the roof and plumbing walls are framed you will cut openings for vents. You can find the location of these openings by dropping a plumb line from the ceiling to just above the cut-off vent pipes.

Using connectors, run the vent pipes up through the roof. Should a roof rafter or other obstruction be in the way, just go around it with ¼ bends (⅛ bends in the drain portion). Cut the vent off 1 foot (.3 m) above the roof. Later, when you place the metal roof flashing over the vent, make sure the roof shingles overlap the flat part of the flashing at the top and sides.

Before you rough frame the bathrooms, you must set all the bathtubs and one-piece showers in place. Generally you need to construct some type of 2 x 4 frame in which to set the bathtub or shower, as shown in Figure 36. When you have completed this, measure for the position of the drain and hook up the trap.

For all other fixtures bring the pipe 1 to 2 inches (2.5–5 cm) beyond where the finished wall will be and cut off the pipe. When the house is almost complete you will connect the fixtures.

THE WATER SUPPLY SYSTEM

Making a Water Supply Plan

On your floor plan start where the water enters the building and roughly sketch in a line to the water heater. From there sketch lines to all areas that need water and connect the fixtures.

You should place your water heater as near the kitchen

All 2 x 4" Framing

Figure 36. **TYPICAL SHOWER STALL FRAMING**

and washing machine as possible, in either the utility room
or a closet. If your bathrooms are located some distance from
the water heater it may take a minute or more to get hot water
to them. In this case you may want to consider installing two
water heaters instead of one. The recommended minimum
size for a water heater is 40 to 50 gallons (151–189 L).

Figuring Out Pipe Sizes

The main cold water line and the line to the water heater should be ¾ inch (1.9 cm) copper pipe. The fixture supply lines and branch line sizes should be selected according to the following table.

Fixture	Fixture Supply Lines, Branch Lines
Lavatory	⅜"
Tub or Shower	½"
Toilet	⅜"
Sink	½"
Garbage Disposal	Uses sink water
Dishwasher	½"
Clothes washer	½"

Where a line serves two or more fixtures make it the larger size. For instance, if a shower and a toilet are on the same line, you must use ½ inch (1.27 cm) copper pipe.

Solder-type and flare-type fittings are generally used. After you have drawn your plan, look it over carefully and make an inventory of the fittings you need. You will probably miss a few fittings but you will come close enough. Simply start at one end of your plan and work to the other.

Making Copper Tubing Connections

You will install the rough plumbing after all walls have been framed and before you put on the wall coverings. If pipes are run in the adobe wall you will have to put these pipes in place as you build the walls. Some adobe builders do this by first installing the pipes, then notching the adobe brick to fit around them.

Generally, if you build your house on a slab you will place the pipes overhead and bring them down to your fixtures through a framed plumbing wall. You could, of course, place the copper pipe under the slab, but you'd have a terrible time getting to these pipes if they started to leak. If you are going to build a wooden floor utilizing joists, you can place your water line underneath the floor in the crawl space.

In installing the water supply line you can use rigid or flexible copper tubing. Flexible tubing is more expensive, but with it you can easily turn corners without using fittings.

In assembling the flexible pipe, use either flare-type or solder-type fittings, depending on your preference. However, you should never use the flare-type fittings inside a wall because of the possibility of leakage.

If you intend to cut a large amount of tubing you will probably want to build a jig in which to cut the pipe square. You can cut both types of pipe with a fine-tooth hacksaw blade. After the tubing is cut remove all burrs with a file.

To make connections using rigid pipe, with steel wool clean and brighten the end of the pipe and the inside of the fitting to be soldered. Apply a thin coat of noncorrosive flux on both the pipe and the fitting.

You will now need an inexpensive Bernzomatic or similar type torch. Heat the pipe by applying the flame directly to the fitting. When the flux bubbles remove the flame, put the fitting and pipe together, and touch the solder to the edge of the fitting.

The solder will flow into the joint immediately. When a line of solder shows completely around the joint, the connection is filled.

If you are using flare-type fittings, slide the flange nut on the tube. Then flare the tube with a flaring or a flanging tool. Now connect the pipes.

When you have installed the pipes in the plumbing wall, extend them a few inches beyond where the finished wall will be, and seal with a cap.

INSTALLING YOUR FIXTURES

When you are ready to install the sinks, place a shutoff valve in each of the hot and cold water lines before connecting these lines to the fixture. For the kitchen and lavatory sinks, the laundry tubs, and the dishwasher, install a trap to stop sewer gases. Connect the garbage disposal.

You can now easily install the toilets, since the floor

flanges are already in place. Some flanges have accommodations for two upright bolts, some for four. Place the bolts in the flange slots.

Turn your toilet bowl upside down. Place a roll of putty completely around the rim and a second roll completely around the discharge opening. You can also use rubber or wax gaskets.

Now install the bowl over the floor flange and twist slightly to settle the putty firmly on the floor. When the bowl is seated, tighten the bolts.

You have, at this point, already framed the bathroom to hold the shower or tub. Now connect the shower and tub drains to the drain pipe.

THE SEPTIC SYSTEM

Where you don't have a sewer to connect to you will need to construct your own sewage system. This system consists of a sewer line, a septic tank, and a distribution field.

A septic tank is a large watertight settling tank that temporarily holds sewage decomposing by bacterial action. Sludge collects at the bottom of the tank, and the liquid flows out into the distribution lines.

A tank can be made of asphalt-coated steel, redwood, concrete, brick, or fiberglass. The cast concrete tanks are the most popular, but many adobe builders are buying the new fiberglass septic tanks. You can build your own concrete tank if you want to take the time, but most people buy them from a contractor who also installs them.

As a general rule (minimum requirement), two-bedroom houses need a 750-gallon (2,819 L) septic tank, a three-bedroom house a 900 gallon (3,407 L) tank, and a four-bedroom house, a 1,000 gallon (3,785 L) tank.

Make the ditches for the drain lines (in the distribution field) 3 feet (.9 m) deep by 18 inches (46 cm) wide. Lay 4-inch (10.2 cm) perforated plastic pipe at about the middle point of each ditch on a gravel bed. Fill the rest of the ditch with dirt. The length of the lines depends on the number of bedrooms in your house and the results of your percolation test (you will need to have a percolation test made by someone authorized by the city, county, or state before you can obtain a permit to put in a septic tank).

The table on page 8 will help you determine the size of the percolation field you will need for your particular house and property. The actual requirements will depend on the rules and regulations of your area's building department.

7
Installing Electrical Wiring

Before you plan the electrical wiring for your home, you should obtain a copy of both the NFPA National Electrical Code (1999 edition) and your local electrical code. You can order a copy of the national code from the National Fire Protection Association, P.O. Box 9101, Quincy, MA 02269. Website: www.catalog.NFPA.org.

Local codes follow the national codes closely, but you will find differences. You can usually pick up a copy of your local code from either the local building department or your power company. Besides the codes, if you intend to wire your own home, you will find the Sears booklet, *Simplified Electrical Wiring*, extremely useful. You can purchase a copy from your nearest Sears store.

PLANNING THE ELECTRICAL SYSTEM

In the planning stage you must decide on the electrical requirements for the entire house. In my own post adobe I planned for what seemed like an overabundance of outlets. Later, living in the house, I was thankful I had included extras for I had outlets handy wherever I needed them. In every room you should space your electrical outlets at least every 12 feet (3.7 m) along the walls. You should avoid at all costs the necessity for stretching a cord across a doorway or under a rug; this can be a serious fire hazard. Install additional outlets instead.

In many homes, there is a ceiling light in every room except the living room. (Lamps plugged into a wall receptacle are generally found in living rooms.) In each room decide how many switches you need to turn the lights on and off. Sometimes, for instance, it is nice to have a switch at each entrance to a room or at both ends of a hall. In the dining room you may want to plan an overhead chandelier controlled by a dimmer switch so you can create a low-light atmosphere.

Adequate lighting is extremely important in the kitchen. This could mean two overhead units utilizing 100-watt bulbs plus an additional 100-watt light over the sink, or two or more four-tube fluorescent units plus an additional two-tube unit over the sink.

In the kitchen also include extra floor outlets and one outlet above the counter for every 4 feet (1.2 m) of counter work area. You might also consider using one or two four-unit kitchen appliance center outlets. These units (simply four receptacles together) help unclutter your working space when you want to plug in several appliances at the same time, such as a toaster, mixer, and coffee maker.

After deciding on your electrical needs in each room, the next step is to take the floor plan you have already drawn, and using the symbols in Figure 37, mark the location of all fixtures. Also show the relationship of all switches to their lighting fixtures. (When two switches control one light they are called three-way switches. When three switches control one light they are called four-way switches.)

You don't have to draw these symbols perfectly on your plans. Just make sure they are legible and that they mark the intended locations of all receptacles, switches, and fixtures. If you wish to make these symbols neater and more uniform you can purchase a small plastic electrical symbol template at an art supply store.

SELECTING WIRE AND BOXES

Copper wire is used today in most electrical installations. Wire size is determined by wire diameter expressed in circular mils.

Figure 37. **ELECTRICAL SYMBOLS**

A circular mil is the cross-sectional area of a circle with a 1 mil or ¹⁄₁₀₀₀ inch (.0254 mm) diameter.

Electrical wire is sized or gauged by the American wire gauge. The most common sizes used in an adobe house are 12 and 14. Heavy-duty circuits require larger sizes. This will be explained under a discussion of individual circuits (page 99). The current capacity, in amperes, of the most common wire sizes and the wire size needed for the various circuits are shown in the following two tables.

Capacity of Copper Wire in Amperes

Wire Size	Capacity in Conduit (amperes)	Capacity in Air (amperes)
14	15	20
12	20	25
10	30	40
8	45	65
6	65	95
4	85	125
3	100	145
2	115	170
1	130	195
0	150	230

Size of Copper Wire Needed for Various Types of Circuits

Circuit	Breaker Size (amperes)	Wire Size
General house	20	12–14
Kitchen-utility appliance circuits	20	12
Garbage disposal	20	12
Dishwasher	20	12
Water heater	30	8
Dryer	30–50	6
Range	50	6
Electric furnace or heat pump	Varies	Varies; check with dealer

WIRING CIRCUITS AND INSTALLING BOXES

Electricity enters the house through the fuse or breaker box (called a distribution or service panel). Circuits run from this panel throughout the house to provide electricity for the out-

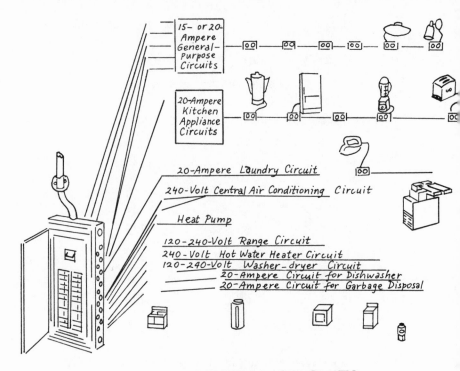

Figure 38. **GENERAL CIRCUITS**

lets, lights, and heavy-duty appliances (Figure 38). Here are the circuits you will need in your house.

- Separate 20-amp general circuits (lights and wall receptacles) for every 500 square feet (465 sq m) of house space, or separate 15-amp general circuits for every 375 square feet (348 sq m) of floor space. You can determine the number of general circuits you will need from your floor plan.
- Two 20-amp grounded appliance circuits, one for the kitchen-dining room and one for the laundry room. These are required by the code and must not be connected to the lighting fixtures.
- Separate 20-amp circuits, one each for the garbage disposal and dishwasher.
- A separate 30-amp circuit for the water heater.
- Separate 50-amp circuits, one each for the dryer, electrical range, and central air conditioning. (Many dryers use only a 30-amp circuit for a standard dryer.)

- A separate circuit for the electric furnace or heat pump. The capacity depends on the unit itself. You will not need this circuit if you utilize a nonelectric heat source.

Before you wire these circuits you must fasten all receptacle, light, junction, and switch boxes in place. You have a choice of either metal or plastic boxes, in common box depths of 2½, 3½, and 1½ inches (6.3, 8.9, and 3.8 cm).

In a conventional frame wall, the code requires that the boxes be positioned so that their front edges are flush with the finished surface. Simply allow the box to extend past the stud the width of the sheetrock—usually ½ inch (1.3 cm). Nail metal boxes to the stud by driving #8 nails through the two side holes of the box. Install plastic boxes by driving ½ inch roofing nails into the stud through the attached hanger strips.

In adobe walls cut a space in the brick for the switch and receptacle boxes. Some builders raise the foundation wall about a foot inside the house and place the outlets in the foundation.

With post adobe, the inner post of a built-up post is grooved and a hole is cut for the receptacle in the outer trimmer (wooden member) (Figure 39). Because of the small space available in a post installation, a 1½ inch (3.8 cm) deep box fits best here.

All receptacle boxes, in both conventional adobe and post adobe construction, are placed approximately 12 inches (31 cm) above the floor. All switch boxes are mounted approximately 54 inches (137 cm) above the floor.

When you start to wire the boxes it is best to do everything strictly according to the code. Unfortunately, practically everyone building his or her own house has a tendency to take shortcuts at this point. In my own case, to reduce expenses I accepted the offer of a friend to wire the house for me "free." The first day he showed up with some aircraft cable, which he proceeded to run throughout the house. When the building inspector saw this innovative "shortcut" he made me take the whole thing out and start over . . . correctly.

Depending on whether you are building a standard adobe or a post adobe, you will be wiring with either Romex

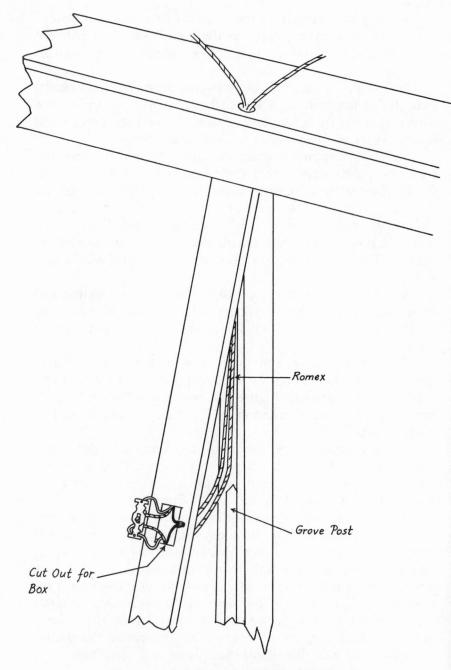

Romex

Grove Post

Cut Out for
Box

Figure 39. **POST ADOBE WIRING**

(indoor-type plastic sheathed cable), thin-wall rigid conduit, or UF (underground feed). Romex has a flat, tough outer plastic jacket and a heavy inner thermo-plastic insulation. You can use Romex anywhere in your house except inside masonry walls. UF cable can be used inside masonry walls and underground. Thin-wall rigid conduit is made of steel with a galvanized finish and must be used inside an adobe wall. All installations should be made with "ground-type" three-wire cable.

To wire the circuits you will need regular carpenter's tools, a tool for cutting and stripping wire, and a conduit bender if you intend to use thin-wall conduit.

When you start to wire the boxes, run Romex from the service panel for each circuit overhead, then make drops to the switches and receptacles. Across the joists, support the Romex on a 1 or 2 inch (2.5 or 5 cm) board or run the cable through holes drilled in the center of the joists. After you have run the wires to the boxes, connect the receptacles, switches, and light fixtures.

Receptacles are available as duplex (double) units and are fitted with "push-in" connector holes in the back so you do not have to bend the wire around a screw terminal. You can buy receptacle plates in many colors to match a decor or in larger sizes to cover up mistakes.

Switches are also available in many different styles and colors and come with screw terminals or "push-in" connections. Besides the standard toggle switch, which operates with an up-and-down lever, you can buy silent switches that don't make a clicking sound, mercury switches, and push-button touch switches. Switches are also available with small lights that enable you to see the switch in the dark.

Light fixtures come in a wide variety of types and styles. Some lighting stores display several hundred fixtures from which to make a selection and will special-order a wide variety of specialty fixtures directly from the manufacturer.

To make the connections in light fixture and junction boxes, use twist-on solderless connectors. Just screw the connector over the wires (see Figure 40).

With a flat-roofed adobe you can run the cable on top of the roof sheathing, underneath the insulation. If you have built a double roof deck for insulation purposes, run the Romex between the decks. In both cases make the drops to the

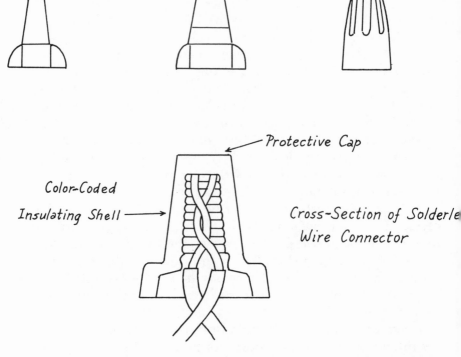

Figure 40. **TWIST-ON SOLDERLESS CONNECTORS**

wall outlets and switches within the conduit. In double wall construction you can run the conduit down the middle of the double rows. The conduit will then be installed as you construct the walls.

Where you intend to plaster the walls, install the conduit by cutting a channel in the adobe wall and the bond beam. When you pour the bond beam you should insert wooden knockout blocks in the concrete bond beam. Leave them in the bond beam until you are ready to install the conduit. Then when you finish the interior walls you will plaster directly over the conduit.

With post adobe construction, bring the Romex down the posts to the receptacle and switch boxes by notching the inner 4 x 4 post with a power saw, or run conduit in the space between the inner post and the bricks.

Inside a conventional stud wall, draw the cable through holes drilled in the center of the stud or notch the stud and fasten metal straps over the notch. With exposed work, strap the cable every 3 feet (.9 m). With concealed work (inside a wall), strap the cable every 4½ feet (11.4 m) and strap within 12 inches (.3 m) of all outlets and switches.

Romex cable must be fastened to the box by either a clamp and lock nut, a built-in cable clamp, or a similar device. Some codes require that all cable be grounded into metal boxes with a ground clip.

For conduit, mount the conduit in place and connect to a steel box (not plastic) with a connector. After the conduit and boxes are installed, pull the wires into the boxes and leave 8 inches (20 cm) of insulated wire at each box. The following table will give you the capacity of the various sizes of conduit.

Conduit Size	Number of Wires Allowed per Conduit
½"	4 #14 or 3 #12 wires
¾"	4 #10, 5 #12, or 3 #8 wires
1¼"	4 #6 or 3 #2, #3, or #4 wires

The most common wiring combinations for wiring switches and light fixtures are shown in Figure 41. If your plans call for two switches or three switches to turn on an overhead fixture, simply hook them up as shown. By using these diagrams you will be able to wire any combination you might need.

WIRING HEAVY-DUTY APPLIANCES

You must install a separate three-wire (sometimes 4-wire), 240-volt circuit for each electric range, electric water heater, electric dryer, central air conditioner, electric furnace, or heat pump.

For the range, wire a 240-volt, 50-amp circuit from the service panel with #6 cable. Install a surface-type receptacle directly to the wall as shown in Figure 42. Next, connect the pigtail to the range terminal by wiring the black wire to the B of the range terminal, the red wire to R, and the white or green to G or W.

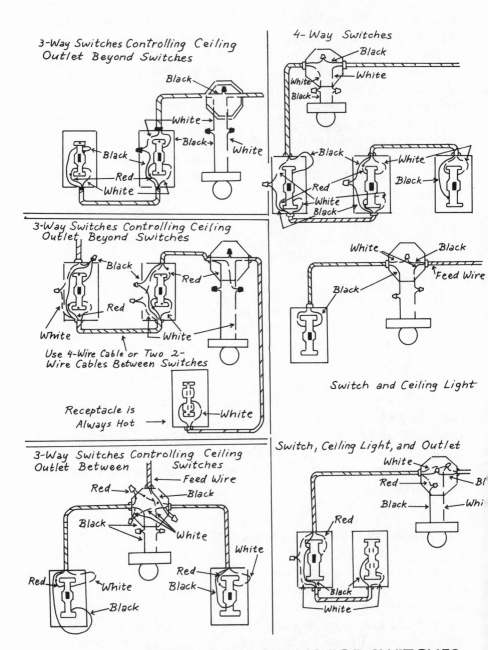

Figure 41. **WIRING DIAGRAMS FOR SWITCHES**

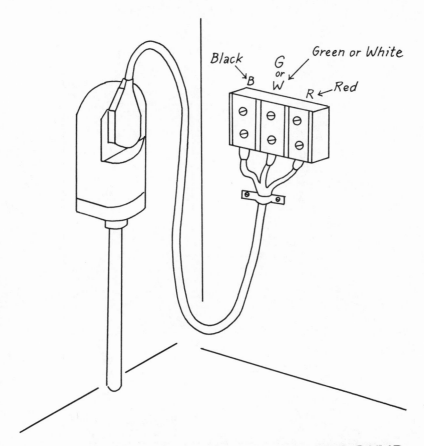

Figure 42. **TYPICAL RANGE OR DRYER HOOKUP**

For a regular electric dryer (4,200 watts), wire a 240/120-volt 30-amp circuit from the service panel with #6 cable. Install a service-type receptacle as before, and connect the pigtail to the dryer the same way you connected the pigtail to the range. For a high-speed dryer (about 8,500 watts) use a 50-amp circuit.

For the water heater, run a separate 30-amp circuit with #8 wire. Most owner-builders install double-element electric water heaters because they produce a more constant supply of hot water. Double-element heaters have two thermostats; the single-element type has one thermostat. Many codes require that you wire first to a safety switch with a breaker near the water heater (see Figure 43).

For air conditioners run a separate 50-amp circuit with #6 or #8 wire.

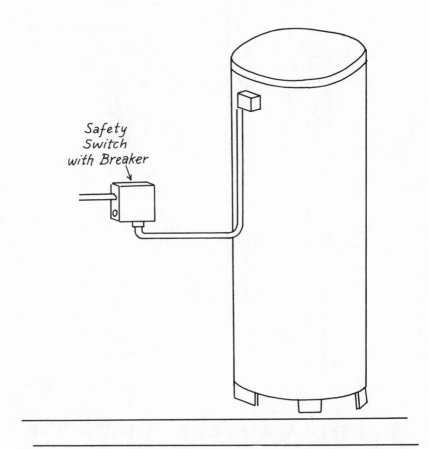

Figure 43. **WATER HEATER WITH SAFETY SWITCH**

INSTALLING THE SERVICE PANEL

Because of the amount of electricity required in most homes today and because you can add to the circuits as you expand your house, I highly recommend that you install a 200-amp service panel. You can buy these panels with the panel and the meter head together as one unit or you may install a separate meter head and service panel. You can also buy 100- to 150-amp panels if you feel these will give you sufficient capacity.

The wires that connect to the electrical company wires (the service drop) are run through an entrance conduit that extends above the roof or underground. You can buy this unit in kit form. The wires from the power pole must be 10 feet (3 m) above the ground and may not come within 3 feet (.9 m) of doors, windows, or other openings.

To install the service panel, first mount the panel in a convenient location. It should be at least three feet from the roof or ceiling, as near the power drop as possible, and where the electric company can read the meter easily. An outside corner near the power pole makes an excellent location. You can also mount it inside a garage if the meter can be reached without difficulty and meets local codes.

To connect the service panel, pull the wires through the conduit. Connect the neutral bare wire to the neutral copper bar called a bus bar in the cabinet as shown in Figure 42. Then connect the two hot wires to the main hubs at the top. These are usually marked mains. The bus bar will have a connector for the ground wire as well as for the neutral wire of all the circuits.

After you have secured the service panel to the wall, installed the entrance conduit, and connected the main wires to the service panel (do not yet connect these wires to the power company wires), then punch out the knockout holes on the side of the panel and bring in the wires from each circuit.

Install a cable clamp in each hole and connect the white wire to the neutral bus bar and the bare ground wire to that same neutral bar. Connect the black wire to the circuit breaker of the proper amps. The black wire is always hot, the white wire neutral.

The final step in connecting the service panel is to install the ground. If you have an underground metal water pipe, ground to this (see Figure 44). If not, install a home-made ground: Use a copper rod ½ inch (1.3 cm) in diameter and at least 8 feet (2.4 m) long, or a ¾ inch (1.9 cm) galvanized iron or steel pipe 8 feet long. Drive the rod 8 feet into the ground and clamp on a #4 bare copper ground wire.

Some localities require that the top of the rod be buried at least 12 inches (30.5 cm) underground and that the rod be located 12 inches from the building. After you have driven the rod or pipe into the ground to the proper depth, connect the copper ground wire to the service panel through the bottom of the box.

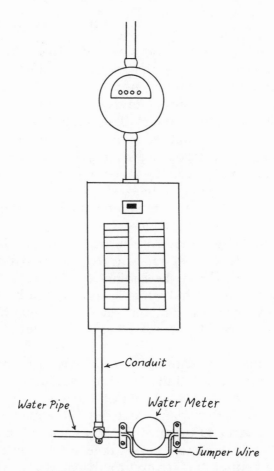

Figure 44. **GROUNDING TO A WATER PIPE**

TESTING AND LABELING THE CIRCUITS

After you have completed your hookups you can test the circuits using an ampmeter. Tape the ends of each circuit together at the main panel, then hook the ampmeter to the contact screws at each outlet. The ampmeter will register if you have a continuous circuit.

You can perform a more complete test using a fairly new device called a receptacle circuit tester (available at hardware and electrical supply stores). Just plug the tester into the receptacles. By interpreting combinations of lit and unlit lights on the tester according to the instructions, you can detect the following seven conditions: (1) a correctly wired circuit, (2) reversed polarity, (3) an open ground, (4) an open neutral, (5) an open hot wire, (6) a reversal of the hot wire and ground, and (7) hot wire is on neutral; the neutral is unwired. If one of these problems is indicated, you simply check back along the circuit until you find the problem.

Most building departments will also require that you mark the circuits (at least in pencil) on the service panel. Do this by trial and error. Station one person in the house, another at the service panel. Start at the top and turn the circuit breakers on and off in order. Have the person in the house tell you which circuit you have turned on (kitchen, bedroom, or whatever). Then write the function of each circuit breaker on the panel.

The easiest way to mark the circuits, of course, is to write the location on the panel when you install them. But most people simply don't take the time at that point and then forget which breaker services which circuit.

Wiring an adobe home is not really very difficult—take it a step at a time. When you're finished you'll have the satisfaction of knowing you did it all yourself.

8
Heating and Cooling Your House

You will find adobe houses heated today by wood stoves, fireplaces, active and passive solar systems, radiant heating, forced-air central heating, wall heaters, and a wide variety of other methods. However, most owner-builders currently utilize either forced-air central heating, radiant heating, some type of solar heating, or a combination of these three methods.

FORCED-AIR CENTRAL HEATING

In a forced-air central heating system, warm air heated by the furnace is forced at high velocity by a fan through ducts to registers located throughout the house. If you install central heating, you will probably use either a Highboy or a Counterflow furnace.

Warm air leaves the Highboy furnace at the top; return air enters through the bottom. The ducts of the Highboy are run through the attic to the registers. This is the easiest central system to install if your adobe house has a pitched roof and if you are building on a concrete slab.

The blower of the Counterflow furnace (Figure 45) is mounted on the bottom so that warm air leaves the furnace at the bottom and return air enters at the top. The air ducts are located in the earth fill under a cement slab, or in the crawl space under a wooden floor. Warm air enters the house through registers located at floor level. Since warm air rises, this type of furnace provides the most efficient heat distribution system.

If you use sheet metal ducts underneath a concrete slab you must encase the ducts in concrete. You may also use Transite air ducts, which are impervious to soil.

Most furnaces today use gas, oil, LP gas, or electricity, but heat pumps are currently becoming more popular as a heat source in a central heating system. Basically, a heat pump operates like a reverse refrigerator. Heat from the air is concentrated by a compressor, while cool air from the house is blown through the air coil where it picks up heat and delivers it to the duct system. In summer this system can be reversed to cool the house.

Planning the Central Heating System

Before trying to install any central heating system you should first lay out the entire plan on paper for your own use. In some cases your local building department will require this.

The first step is to make an additional copy of your floor plan. On this plan locate a place near the center of the house for the furnace and the furnace room.

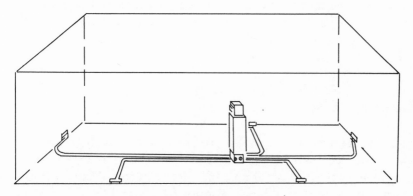

Figure 45. COUNTERFLOW FURNACE

Next, locate the register outlets, on paper, in each room. The preferred location is at the outer edge of the house. Your choice of register types is discussed on page 110.

Now, on paper, connect the ducts from the furnace to the registers (Figure 46). You have a choice of two systems. In the *round pipe radial system,* the pipes (ducts) radiate from the furnace to the duct outlets. This is least expensive and works efficiently in a house of under 1,500 square feet (135 sq m). The alternative is the *extended-plenum system.* A plenum is a sheet metal box that fits on the top and bottom of the furnace either to distribute the warm air or to return the cold air to the furnace. An extended-plenum unit utilizes a wide, flat sheet metal duct that extends outward from the furnace in one or both directions. Round duct pipes take the warm air from the extended plenum directly to the registers. This system is used in many houses over 1,500 square feet (135 sq m) because the large, flat duct offers less resistance to air movement than do the smaller round ducts.

The dealer from whom you buy your furnace can help you decide what BTUH (British Thermal Units per Hour) capacity your particular furnace should have. This will depend on the size of your house and how it is insulated.

Most mail-order houses (such as Sears and Montgomery Ward) will plan the heating installation for you and tailor the ductwork to your particular house. Large local plumbing and heating firms will also make the plenum and ductwork to the specifications indicated on your plans. In my own case I bought a heat pump, a register, and all the ductwork from a heating engineer who specialized in do-it-yourself installations. He designed the entire system to fit my house and then made periodic visits while I was installing it to make sure that I was doing it correctly.

Installing the System

Make sure that you install your furnace on a solid, level base and that you build the furnace room large enough so that there is sufficient air for proper combustion. Many building codes require that a furnace room be made 12 inches (31 cm) wider than the furnace, with at least 3 inches (8 cm) of work-

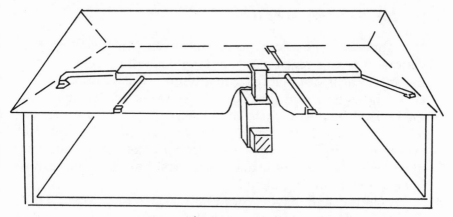

Extended plenum System in Attic
Highboy Furnace

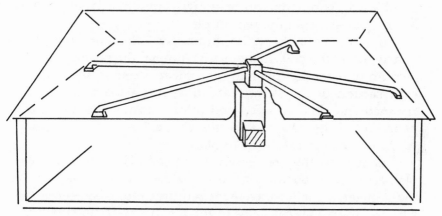

Round Pipe Radial System
Highboy Furnace

Figure 46. **OVERHEAD CENTRAL HEATING**

ing space along the back and top and 6 inches (15 cm) of working space across the front.

The easiest way to install the warm air outlets is to fasten the register boots or "holders" in place before you close the walls or ceiling. Generally you nail blocks between the joists or studs around the sheet metal boot, then nail that boot directly to the wooden blocks.

There are, however, some differences in installing the various types of registers. A rectangular ceiling register, for instance, has a face that fits into a ceiling register boot. To install this register you first nail blocks to the joists, then nail the register boot directly to the blocks.

A round ceiling register also fits into a boot, but the ceiling boot fits into a square mounting plate. To install, you must nail the mounting plate into position, then place the boot in the mounting plate.

Wall registers have a face that attaches to a box called a stackhead. To install, simply nail the stackhead in place at the desired height. Floor registers consist of a face that fits into a pan. If you have installed the ducts underneath the concrete slab, you must set the duct system and the floor register pans in place before you pour the slab. For wooden floors over a crawl space, simply cut an opening in the floor large enough for the pan and nail the pan in place.

In most central heat distribution systems, the round, 6 to 8 inch (15.2–20.3 cm) diameter sheet metal ducts attach to the plenum or extended plenum by a collar. In its simplest form, each section of the sheet metal duct has a plain end and a crimped end. The crimped end of one section fits inside the plain end of the next section, forming a simple airtight joint. A screw holds the sections in place.

Radial ducting is easiest to install. The ducts (as explained) extend outward from a boxlike warm-air plenum to the registers. This arrangement requires the least number of elbows. To install, cut holes in the plenum with tin snips, insert collars in the holes, and attach the ductwork to the collars.

The extended plenums (large, rectangular metal ducts) can extend in both directions from the furnace the length of the house. They are generally made 8 inches deep and 10 to 24 inches wide (20 cm deep and 25–70 cm wide). The round pipe ducts branch off from this extended plenum to warm-air registers. To install, cut holes in the extended plenum at the takeoff points indicated on your heating plan, insert collars in these holes, and attach the ductwork to these collars.

To secure the extended plenum and the ductwork, you must support the extended plenum every 2 feet (.6 m) with hangers and the pipe duct every 10 feet (3.1 m) with pipe hangers. You can obtain these hangers from any plumbing and heating supply store.

Since all uninsulated sheet metal ductwork loses heat along its entire run, you must insulate all ductwork with at least a 1 inch (2.5 cm) blanket of standard duct insulation.

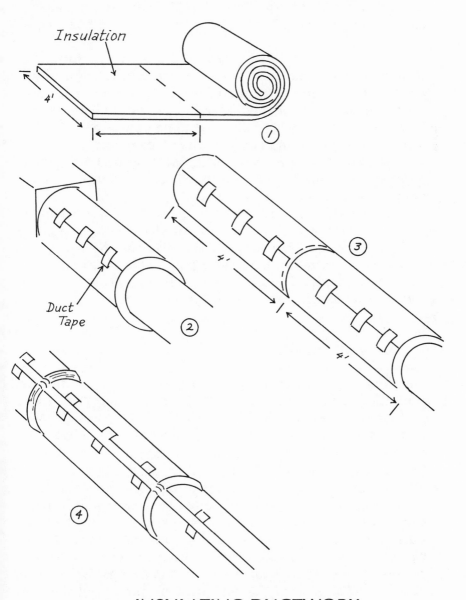

Figure 47. **INSULATING DUCTWORK**

Duct insulation generally comes in rolls. To install, first cut the insulation as shown in Figure 47 so that it will wrap completely around the ducts. Determine the width of the strips to be cut this way: Measure the circumference of the round duct in inches with a steel tape. If you are using 1 inch insulation, add 6½ inches (16 cm) to the measured circumference. If you are using 2 inch (5 cm) insulation, add 13 inches (33 cm).

For rectangular ducts, measure the perimeter (distance around the duct) in inches. If you are using 1 inch insulation, add 9 inches (23 cm) to the perimeter measurement. If you are using 2 inch insulation, add 17 inches (43 cm) to the perimeter measurement. After you have wrapped the ducts with the insulation, secure it in place with duct tape (Figure 47).

Besides warm-air ducts, all furnaces need some sort of return-air system. This usually consists of a return-air plenum, ductwork, and a return-air grill.

Generally the grill is located in the wall and a rectangular duct is run from there to the return-air plenum. If you are installing a Highboy furnace, you can place the furnace on a raised base and make that base a part of the return-air system. Several types of return-air installations for both Highboy and Counterflow furnaces are shown in Figure 48.

RADIANT HEATING

For floor-type radiant heating, soft copper pipe or rubber tubing is embedded in the concrete foundation slab when the slab is poured, and the pipe is hooked up to a small water boiler. Hot water circulating in the floor heats the house.

Some builders also use radiant baseboard heating. Water from a boiler runs under the floor in copper pipes to circulating baseboard heaters located along the exterior walls. You can also use electric wall panels or electric baseboard heaters either with individual built-in thermostats, several thermostats to control the temperature in different areas of the house, or one thermostat for the entire house. Small adobe houses sometimes are heated with one or two gas or oil wall heaters, which generally are adequate in warmer climates.

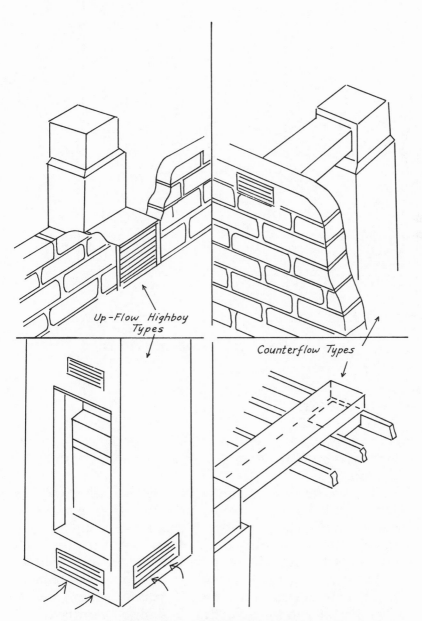

Figure 48. **VARIOUS TYPES OF RETURN-AIR INSTALLATIONS**

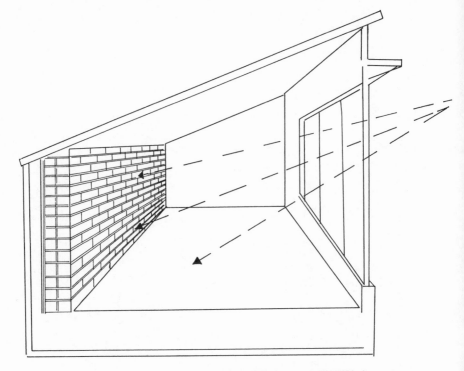

Figure 49. **PASSIVE SOLAR SYSTEM**

SOLAR HEATING

You can partially heat an adobe house with the sun's energy using a passive solar system (direct-gain heating) or an active solar system.

The passive system (Figure 49) utilizes a large window facing south to allow the winter sun to penetrate into the living area. An overhang keeps the higher summer sun from entering the house. An extra-thick adobe wall stores the sun's energy and later redistributes that energy in the form of heat.

An active solar heating system consists of panels of metal or glass to trap the sun's heat (called collector plates), a water tank or rock bins to store that heat, and pipes or ducts to convey it to wherever heat is needed. This system requires thermostats, fans, pumps, and valves to control the house temperature and to distribute the heat throughout the house.

The flat collector utilizes a metal plate, called an absorber plate, made of aluminum, copper, or steel that is painted a flat black. The absorber plate is housed in a shallow wooden or metal box covered with transparent glass or fiberglass. The short-wave solar radiation penetrates the glass or fiberglass, but the long waves reflected by the absorber plate cannot pass back through the glass and are trapped inside.

When the temperature of the collector becomes 20° to 30° warmer than the house, a differential thermostat turns on a pump to circulate some type of heat transfer fluid through the collectors. The fluid is heated in the collectors, then transferred back to the heat storage. When the heat is needed, another thermostat turns on a fan that draws heat from the storage area to warm the house in extended cloudy weather.

You will need some type of backup system, such as individual electric wall heaters, a fireplace, a wood stove, or something similar. For detailed information on the wide variety of solar systems available today, consult one or more of the solar energy books listed in the Bibliography.

COOLING AN ADOBE HOUSE

For cooling your adobe house you have a choice among evaporative coolers, single-room refrigerator air conditioners, and central air conditioning.

An evaporative cooler works this way: a pump supplies water to saturate absorbent pads. A fan draws outside air through these pads on the sides of the unit, and the evaporation of the water reduces the temperature of the air that enters the house. The evaporative cooler works reasonably well in areas of low humidity such as the desert. In high humidity areas, however, refrigerator air conditioning is almost a must.

Refrigerator air conditioning room units come in several sizes and can cool a small house or one or two rooms. The advantage of these single units is that they can be mounted quickly in a window or placed in a wall opening with very little effort.

If you intend to cool more than a few rooms or have a fairly large house you will find a central air conditioning system much more practical. You can install central air conditioning in your central heating system when you build your house, or you may wait and install it later. A cooling coil is generally installed in the plenum or an extension of it so that the regular heating system blower drives the air for summer cooling.

When selecting a cooling system, figure, as a rule-of-thumb, 1 ton of cooling capacity (12,000 BTU) for each 500 square feet (45 sq m) of floor area.

A split system air conditioner is usually installed with central air conditioning because it isn't practicable to mount a single large unit within the central system. The split system consists of a coil inside the house and a condenser and compressor outside, with copper tubing connecting the two parts. The cooling coil, condenser, and connecting tubing are charged with refrigerant and sealed. When the tubing is connected to the components, a cutter inside the fitting breaks the seal between the tubing and the component to which it is being connected. When all connections are made the refrigerant flows throughout the system.

All air conditioning requires the movement of a large volume of air. This means that ducts used for both heating and cooling must be larger than ducts used for heating alone. These larger ducts should be installed when you make your initial heating installation. The dealer from whom you purchase your central heating system can help you with this.

While most heating and air conditioning installations today are made by contractors, in reality it is a very uncomplicated process. With the information in this chapter and a little help from your local supplier, you ought to be able to do all your own work with very little difficulty.

9

Building Your Adobe Fireplace

Nothing really sets off an adobe house like a fireplace. Some adobe builders construct a large fireplace at one end of a living room. Others insist on a fireplace in every room, and others build their fireplaces to suit the individual style of the home they are constructing.

TYPES OF FIREPLACES

While there are literally hundreds of exterior fireplace styles from which to choose, the following are the major types.

The *wall fireplace* is the most common type found in an adobe house and is simply a fireplace built into one wall. The face of this fireplace can incorporate an entire wall or simply a small portion of it. On an inner wall you will need to allow space inside the house for the fireplace depth. In an outer wall, the fireplace can extend outside the house.

The *back-to-back fireplace* design is extremely practical when you have two rooms with a common wall, such as a living room or den, and you wish to put a fireplace in each room. Both fireplaces can use the same chimney and overall masonry structure, but each will require a separate flue.

Two-way fireplaces have opposite faces or two opposite fire openings in different rooms. This type of fireplace makes

Figure 50. An exposed adobe fireplace. The interior of this fireplace is lined with firebrick. The facing is finished with adobe brick.

a good room divider, while at the same time giving the two rooms a "joined" feeling.

The *three-way fireplace* opens on three sides and projects into the room like a peninsula, where its sides often form part of a hall between rooms. You can purchase special dampers that make both two-sided and three-sided fireplaces easy to construct.

The *hooded prefabricated fireplace* looks good with adobe and is more efficient than a conventional fireplace because the metal hood radiates a great deal of heat. These fireplaces can be installed as free-standing units on legs, or they can be mounted on or near a wall.

The *standard Kiva fireplace* (Figure 51), which is traditional in many Southwest homes, generally resembles a small, rounded, stuccoed beehive.

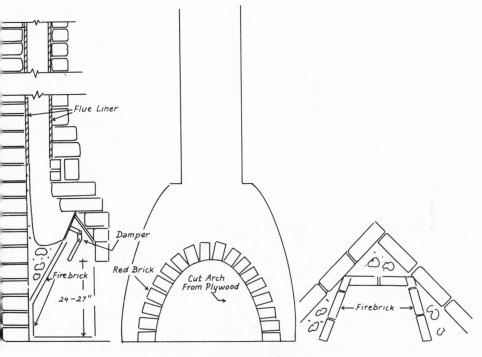

Figure 51. **KIVA TYPE FIREPLACE**

DESIGNING YOUR FIREPLACE

To plan the appearance of your fireplace it will help you to look through several home-planning books, such as *A Portfolio of Fireplace Ideas* (Creative Publishing International), *Adobe: Remodeling of Fireplaces* (Sunstone Press), and *House Beautiful Fireplaces* (Hearst Books). You will also find good illustrations of traditional Kiva fireplaces in *Build with Adobe* (The Swallow Press, Inc.).

In designing your fireplace you will need to decide on the size of the opening. Basically the opening should fit the room in which the fireplace is to be built; if the opening is too big or too small in relation to the size of the room, the fireplace will look inappropriate.

The height of the fireplace opening is usually ⅔ to ¾ of the width. The following is a table of room sizes with suggested widths for appropriate fireplace openings.

Size of Room (ft)	Width of Fireplace Opening (in)	
	Short Wall	Long Wall
10 × 14	24	24–32
12 × 16	28–36	32–36
12 × 20	32–36	36–40
14 × 28	32–40	40–48
16 × 30	36–40	48–60
20 × 36	40–48	48–72

Laying Out Your Fireplace on Paper

On the plans you submit, all building departments require that you show the chimney and fireplace details. Since most fireplaces are similar internally, it isn't that hard to draw plans even though you don't know the first thing about it. Simply take a standard fireplace plan and modify it to fit whatever fireplace design you have in mind (Figures 52, 53).

BUILDING YOUR FIREPLACE

Before you start to construct the fireplace, you must build a concrete fireplace foundation that will be at least 12 inches (31 cm) thick and 4 inches (10 cm) wider and longer than the fireplace itself. The foundation must rest on solid, undisturbed soil and must be reinforced with ½ inch (1.3 cm) #4 rebar, running both ways, and laid on 12 inch centers. If the ground freezes in winter you must place this foundation below the frost level.

If you build your house on a concrete slab, dig down deep enough at the fireplace location to allow 12 inches of concrete to be poured for the fireplace foundation. Reinforce this foundation with rebar as you would for a freestanding foundation.

If you have some sort of crawl space under the house you will need to build a *stem* (a concrete structure between the

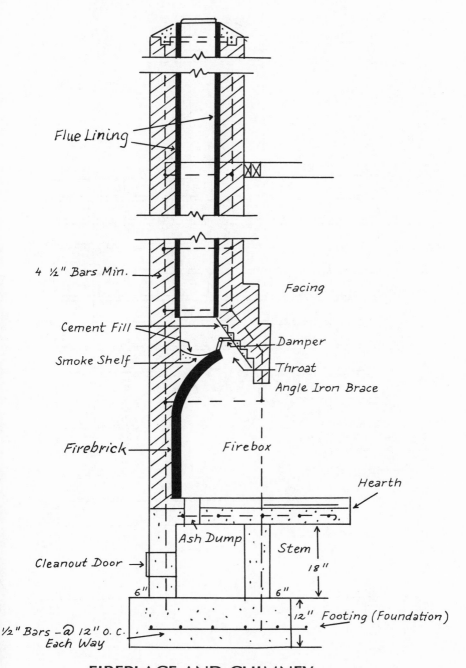

Figure 52. **FIREPLACE AND CHIMNEY** (side section)

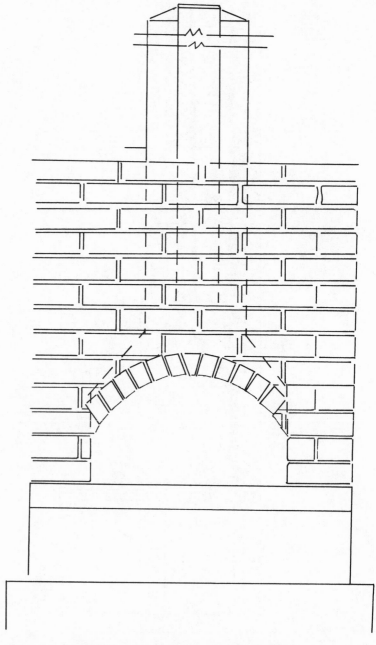

Figure 53. **FIREPLACE AND CHIMNEY** (front section)

foundation and the firebox) up to the floor level. Some sort of ashpit or ash dump should be provided in the stem, as shown in Figure 52. You will not need a stem if you are building your fireplace on a concrete slab.

The *firebox* (the place where you build the fire) should be made of hard brick especially designed for lining the interior of fireplaces. Lay this brick up with fired clay mortar, allowing a maximum joint thickness of ¼ inch (.6 cm) between the bricks.

Make the back wall of the firebox vertical for approximately 12 inches (31 cm), and then slant the wall forward to the *throat* (the top of the firebox). Angle the side walls 3 to 5 inches (8–13 cm) for each foot of depth. The outer shell of the fireplace consists of a masonry wall built around the firebox. Many codes require a 12 inch thickness between the inside of the firebox and the exterior of the shell. The throat should always be as wide as the firebox and 4 to 5 inches (10–13 cm) deep.

When you slanted the firebox toward the throat you created a space between the firebricks and the back wall of the chimney. Fill this space with mortar and scrap pieces and make it concave at the top as shown in Figure 52. This area now becomes the *smoke shelf*. This shelf redirects downdrafts back up the chimney and keeps smoke from blowing out the front of the fireplace.

You are now ready to install the *damper*. Most dampers have flanges that allow them to be seated directly on the brick you have laid up. The back edge of the damper should rest on the forward edge of the smoke shelf. The joint between the damper and the bottom of the smoke shelf should be sealed with cement fill so the flames can only reach the flue through the damper throat (Figure 52).

Many owner-builders today buy a prefab metal unit incorporating the throat and the damper. This is the easiest way to get it right if you haven't built a fireplace before.

Because the fireplace at the throat level is so much wider and longer than the *flue liner* that you will install next, it will be necessary to start reducing its dimensions at this point. Do this by reverse stair-stepping (corbelling) the brick courses. Simply overlap each brick by about 1 inch (2.5 cm). The chamber above the damper that results from the corbelling of the bricks is called the *smoke chamber.*

Use firebrick wherever the brick comes in contact with the inner heat; otherwise use regular brick. Make sure that your masonry work is smooth on the inside so soot cannot collect. When you reach the proper height make a ledge in the chimney on which to rest the flue liner.

The *flue* in a fireplace is the opening up the chimney that allows smoke to escape. The easiest way to build a flue is to buy and install either a round or a rectangular vitrified clay flue liner.

The cross-section opening of a flue liner should be $1/10$ (some builders say from $1/8$ to $1/12$) the area of the fireplace opening. If you have a 30 by 40 inch (76 x 102 cm) fireplace opening, the area of the opening is 1,200 square inches (7,752 sq cm). One tenth of this is 120 square inches (775 sq cm). A flue liner that measures 10 by 12 inches (25 x 31 cm) will satisfy this cross-sectional area requirement.

The following table will give you a handy guide for determining the depth and the flue liner sizes for your fireplace.

| Size of Fireplace Opening | | | Size of Flue Lining Required | |
| | | | Standard Rectangular (outside) | Standard Round (inside) |
Width (in)	Height (in)	Depth (in)	Dimensions (in)	Diameter (in)
24	24	16–18	8½ × 13	10
28	24	16–18	8½ × 13	10
30	28–30	16–18	8½ × 13	10
36	28–30	16–18	8½ × 13	12
42	28–32	16–18	13 × 13	12
48	32	18–20	13 × 13	15
54	36	18–20	13 × 18	15
60	36	18–20	13 × 18	15
54	40	20–22	13 × 18	15
60	40	20–22	18 × 18	18
66	40	20–22	18 × 18	18
72	40	22–28	18 × 18	18

After you have put the flue liner in place with firebrick mortar, you can now build the chimney. It should be at least 6 inches (15 cm) thick from the top of the smoke chamber to the top of the flue. Use either regular bricks or hollow concrete blocks reinforced with four ½ inch (1.3 cm) strips of rebar. (See Chapter 5 for instructions on how to lay up brick.)

Most codes specify that no woodwork should come in contact with the chimney and that a 1 to 2 inch (2.5–5 cm) space be left between the walls of the chimney and the wooden beams. The space between the wooden framing and the chimney walls can be filled with noncombustible materials. Some codes also require that you strap the fireplace chimney to the joists at the ceiling line with 3/16 by 1 inch (1.2 x 2.5 cm) steel straps.

If the chimney is to be left exposed above the roof, you should build this portion with stabilized adobe bricks. If you intend to plaster the exterior of the chimney, then use either adobe bricks or concrete blocks.

You will need to install flashing where the chimney goes through the roof. Galvanized base strips should be fitted to the roof, bent up against the chimney, and sealed in place against the roof with mastic. You can obtain flashing from a building supply dealer.

Next take counterflashing (additional sheet metal strips), insert them in the joints between the bricks, and bend them downward over the base strips. Each strip of flashing should overlap the one below as you proceed up the slant of the roof. The joints created where the counterflashing overlaps the base strips should be soldered together the same way you soldered copper pipe (see Chapter 6, page 77).

The final step in building your chimney is to add the *chimney cap*. Make this cap of 2 inch (5 cm) thick concrete (not mortar) and slope it from the flue lining to the outside of the chimney.

You are now ready to give your fireplace its personality by finishing the *face*—the exterior portion of the fireplace that you actually see inside the room. You can make the face of brick, stone, adobe bricks, stucco, or similar materials. I personally feel that adobe bricks make the best possible fireplace facing for an adobe house. Lay up these bricks as you would for any adobe wall.

If you wish to construct an arched opening for your fireplace, cut a plywood arch, then lay the adobe bricks over this arch as shown in Figure 51. If constructed correctly, the key—the wedge-shaped pieces of brick (see Figure 53)—will support the arch and all the weight above it.

When I built my fireplace, I didn't trust my own ability. I bought several pieces of heavy steel and laid these just above the arch to support the weight of the bricks. In a traditional Kiva fireplace, these arches are constructed of regular bricks.

To finish your fireplace you will need to build a *hearth*. A hearth is a noncombustible area around the fireplace that is required by most codes. A hearth can be flush with the floor or raised, and should be built 16 to 18 inches (41–46 cm) wide and any length you like, directly in front of the firebox.

CIRCULATING FIREPLACES

A circulating fireplace is a prefabricated, double-walled metal firebox unit that increases your fireplace's efficiency. Air, heated in an air chamber between the inner and outer steel walls of the circulating fireplace, is usually returned to heat the room through grills in the front of the fireplace itself. It is also possible to funnel this hot air into the ducts of your heating system, thereby using the fireplace to supplement the overall house heat.

This system turns the fireplace from a very inefficient heat producer to an extremely efficient one. Complete instruction sheets specifying the flue sizes and all other dimensions are enclosed with each unit.

10

Framing and Covering the Roof

You will find four roof styles used by most adobe house builders today: the flat roof, the gable, the hip, and the shed (Figure 54). The style you select depends on the type of adobe house you are building, the way that style fits into the surrounding area, and your own personal preference.

The *flat roof* seems especially appropriate for the Southwest, where it blends well with many similar traditional adobe houses. The flat roofs of most houses in this area use vigas, traditional round, peeled logs, or a rectangular roof beam to support the roof. Vigas are currently widely available from dealers in the Southwest. (See Appendix for listings.)

A *gable roof* is a sloping or pitched roof that has an equal slope from one end to the other. Each end of this type of roof forms a triangle or gable with the end wall. Gable roofs are frequently used with Western ranch-style adobes.

A *hip roof* slopes to the house walls on all sides. This type of roof is especially appropriate for an adobe house that is built around a courtyard. It is also used when you want an extended roofline to protect the entire house from the sun or the rain.

Shed roofs are really flat roofs that are higher at one end than the other. They may be used effectively on a hillside where you intend to build the house on two levels. They are

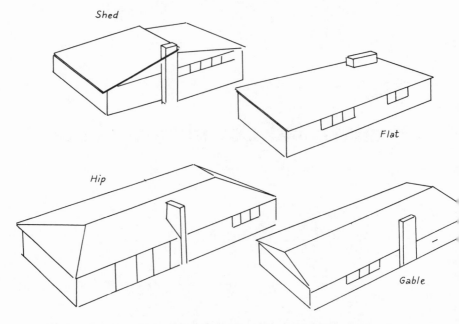

Figure 54. **BASIC TYPES OF ROOFS**

also often used to provide skylight windows between the roofs to provide additional light inside the house.

PUTTING THE ROOF PLAN ON PAPER

To obtain a building permit you will need to include a roof plan with your other sheets. Start by drawing an outline of your roof (as viewed from above). Next show the rectangular beams, vigas, joists (the members that span the roof at the top of the wall), and the rafters (members placed at an angle to give the roof its pitch). Which of these members you use will depend on the type of roof you build.

Identify all members by grade and size, obtaining these figures from tables furnished by most building departments. Also show typical cross sections through the roof. These are not needed for a flat roof. On most roof plans you will show only one or two rafters, joists, or beams per section.

The following tables will give you rough spacing for vigas, beams, floor joists, and rafters.

Size of Vigas for Various Roof Spans

Diameter of Viga (in)	Maximum Roof Span (ft)
6	10
8	16
10	20

Size of Beams for Various Roof Spans
(20 lbs per sq ft live load, spacing 4–6 ft on center)

Size of Beam (in)	Maximum Roof Span (ft)
4 × 6	10
4 × 8	12
4 × 10	14
4 × 10	16
4 × 10	18
6 × 10	20
6 × 12	22

Allowable Spans for Ceiling Joists
(10 lbs per sq ft live load, spacing 16 in on center)

Size of Joist (in)	Douglas Fir Grades		
	3	2	1
2 × 4	9' 4"	11' 6"	11' 9"
2 × 6	14' 7"	18' 1"	18' 5"
2 × 8	19' 3"	23' 10"	24' 10"
2 × 10	24' 7"	30' 5"	31' 0"

Allowable Spans for Rafters
(20 lbs per sq ft live load, spacing 16 in on center)

Size of Rafter (in)	Douglas Fir Grades		
	3	2	1
2 × 6	9' 4"	12' 4"	13' 7"
2 × 8	12' 3"	16' 3"	17' 10"
2 × 10	15' 8"	20' 8"	22' 10"
2 × 12	19' 0"	25' 2"	27' 9"

These tables are intended as general guidelines only. Load limits are established by local building codes. Check with your local building department for the span tables used in your area. You can also obtain plank and beam framing tables plus additional plank and beam information by writing for the pamphlet *Wood Construction Data No. 4, Plank and Beam Framing*, National Forest Products Association, Technical Services Division, 1619 Massachusetts Ave., N.W., Washington, D.C. 20036.

FRAMING THE ROOF

To install any type of roof you will need to anchor a treated plate (a wooden member like a 2 x 4 or 2 x 6) on top of the bond beam. Do this by placing anchor bolts on 4 foot (1.2 m) centers in the bond beam when you pour the concrete, then drill holes in the 2 x 4 or 2 x 6 plate at the appropriate places and bolt the plate to the bond beam.

As an alternative for securing vigas or beams, you can insert plumber's tape or galvanized straps in the bond beam when it is poured, then nail the members to the tape or straps. For a post adobe frame, simply nail the top plates directly to the header beam.

Framing the Flat Roof

Vigas (the traditional round, peeled logs) have been used for many years in the Southwest for roofing adobe homes. Most builders place the butt ends on the same side of the house to form a natural slope for water drainage.

If you intend to use vigas you should trim off all large irregularities so that you can nail a relatively flat deck on top. Place the crown—the high part of the bend in the viga—with the bend up.

If you use roof beams instead of vigas, set them in place and anchor them to the bond beam with plumber's tape (as explained), or anchor the roof beams to bolts placed in the bond beam before the concrete is poured.

It is also possible to frame a flat roof with joists placed on 16 inch (41 cm) centers and nailed directly to the top plate.

Figure 55. A post adobe house utilizes a conventional frame roof. The rafters are cut on the ground to predetermined measurements, then nailed in place on the roof.

This is probably the easiest way to frame a flat roof, since both vigas and beams are so heavy considerable effort is sometimes required to lift them to the top of the wall.

Framing a Gable Roof

The essential parts of a gable roof are the *joists* (members laid across the top of the walls), the *ridgeboard* (the top member of the roof that runs the length of a gable roof), and the *common rafters* (diagonal members of the same length that run from the lower edge of the roof to the ridgeboard). Always make the ridgeboard one size larger than the rafters.

Cut and nail the joists as shown in Figure 56. The rafters must now be cut to fit your particular house. Actually the total length of the rafter and the angles of all the cuts depend on the pitch of your roof. The pitch is the angle of the roof expressed in the number of inches the roof rises as it moves 12 inches (30.5 cm) horizontally. The pitch of a roof that rises 4 inches (10.2 cm) upward over a 12 inch horizontal distance is expressed as 4/12.

You can lay out the angles and measurements of all common rafters using either a steel square or readily available rafter tables. To do this you will need to know the span of the house and the run. The span is simply the building width (from outer wall to outer wall) and the run is one-half the span.

Now let's try one. To lay out a common rafter for a house with a 4/12 roof pitch, mark 4 inches on the tongue of a steel square and 12 inches on the body (Figure 57). The diagonal distance between the two marks will be one unit.

If you want to lay out a rafter for a house with a span of 20 feet (6.1 m) and a run of 10 feet (3.1 m), mark off ten units with your square on the rafter. This gives you the distance from the top of the rafter to the outer edge of the house (the line of rafter). For a 2 foot (.6 m) overhang, simply mark off two more units. You must now subtract ¾ inch (1.9 cm) from the top end of the rafter to allow for the width of the ridgeboard.

Now, using the square as shown (Figure 57), draw lines on the rafters at the top and bottom ends for the saw cuts. Mark the seat cut (a piece cut out of the rafter at the wall so that rafter will fit the top of the wall). When you have made these cuts, you will have a rafter of the correct length (for the span of the house) with all cuts made at the proper angles to fit the other members.

While some builders frame a roof this way, the easiest way to lay out the rafters is to look up all the measurements in the tables provided in *The Full Length Roof Framer Book*, available from A.F.V. Riechers. Order by phone: 1 800-859-3669. This

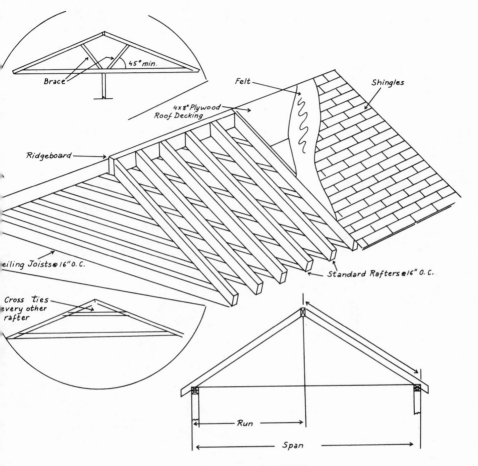

Figure 56. **GABLE ROOFS**

book provides rafter measurements for roof pitches varying from ½/12 to 24/12. To lay out the rafter you simply look up the lengths and the overhang in the tables. Instructions provided with these tables show you exactly how to make all calculations.

Once you have made one pair of common rafters, take them up on the roof and check to make sure they fit. Now, with one of these rafters as a model, cut all the remaining common rafters (they are placed every 16 inches on center). You do not have to make any more measurements since all rafters in a gable roof are the same size.

To put the rafters in place you will need two people. Nail the ridgeboard at one end of the house between two rafters. Temporarily support the other end. Mark the ridgeboard

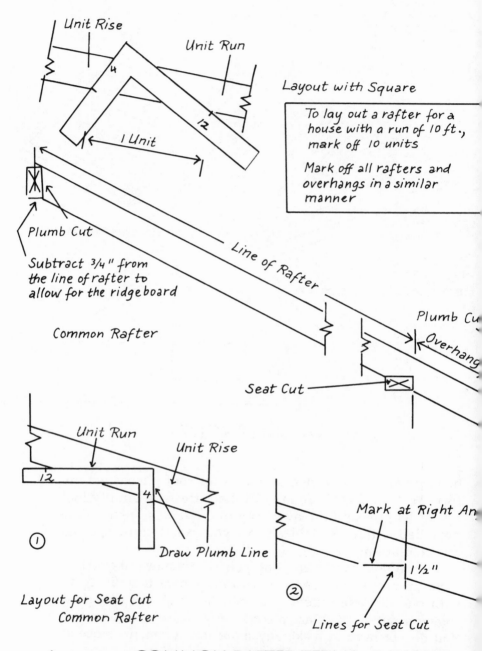

Unit Rise

Unit Run

1 Unit

Layout with Square

To lay out a rafter for a house with a run of 10 ft., mark off 10 units

Mark off all rafters and overhangs in a similar manner

Plumb Cut

Subtract 3/4" from the line of rafter to allow for the ridge board

Common Rafter

Line of Rafter

Plumb Cu

Overhang

Seat Cut

Unit Run

Unit Rise

12

4

Draw Plumb Line

①

Layout for Seat Cut
Common Rafter

Mark at Right An

1 ½"

②

Lines for Seat Cut

Figure 57. **COMMON RAFTER TERMS—LAYOUT**

every 16 inches on center. Nail the rafters in place on these marks as you proceed down the roof and add ridgeboard as you need it.

This is the basic framing structure. You will also need collar ties and rafter braces. Check with your local building department for size and location.

If you prefer not to frame the roof in this manner you can buy ready-made fabricated trusses. These trusses are preengineered and save a considerable amount of time in erecting the roof.

Framing a Hip Roof

A hip roof slopes downward to all walls, as shown in Figure 58. To frame this type of roof you need (in addition to common rafters) the following types of rafters.

A *hip rafter* is needed wherever two slopes meet. The hip rafter runs from the edge of the ridgeboard to an outer corner.

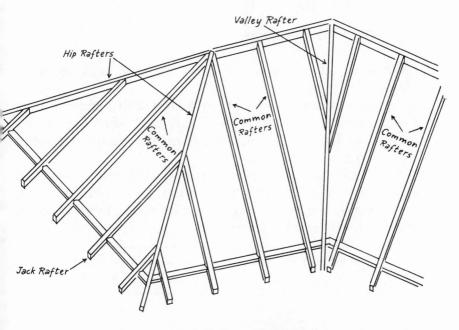

Figure 58. **HIP ROOF FRAMING**

A *valley rafter* is needed wherever two roofs intersect and runs from a ridge to an interior corner.

Jack rafters extend from the edge of the roof to either a hip or a valley rafter.

Cut the ends and seat of the hip, valley, and jack rafters as shown. You can determine the exact sizes using the tables in *The Full Length Roof Framer Book.*

To frame the hip roof, put up the ridgeboard and common rafters as with the gable roof. Add the common rafters at the end of each ridgeboard, then nail in the hip and valley rafters. Mark the location of the jack rafters as shown (Figure 58), then cut and nail them in place. Finally add the remaining common rafters.

An alternative method is to lay out the common rafters with a square and frame them first. By projecting along the edges of the common rafters, you can measure the exact length of all hip and valley rafters with a tape measure. After the valley and hip rafters are nailed in place, mark and measure for the jack rafters. As I know from experience, this is the slowest of the two methods.

COVERING THE ROOF

Once you have framed the roof you will need to cover (sheath) it.

You can cover 1 inch flat roof beams with 2 inch (5 cm) or thicker wooden planking. The maximum allowable span for 2 inch 2 x 6 planking is 8 feet (2.7 m) over two supports, 6 feet (1.8 m) over a single span.

You can also use preformed roof decking to cover a flat roof. This planking comes in 2 x 8 foot (.6 m x 2.7 m) sheets with tongue-in-grooved edges. The following table gives spacing for several thicknesses.

Minimum Thickness (in.)	Maximum Beam Spacing (in.)
1½	24
2	32
3	48

Traditional Southwestern adobe houses also use the latilla, a peeled pole of about 1 to 2 inches in diameter, or cedros, split cedar poles. Both are laid diagonally between the beams to create a herringbone pattern.

You can insulate this decking by adding rigid insulation on top of the decking or by placing fiberglass or similar insulation on top of the deck and then building a second deck over it. Several possibilities are shown in Figure 59.

After you have placed decking on a flat roof you will need to waterproof it. To do this, first apply several layers of asphalt felt paper, using hot melted asphalt between the layers. You can rent a tar kettle at most local rental yards. When the asphalt between the layers cools, flood the top of the roof with hot asphalt and embed 1 to 2 inches (2.5–5 cm) of small gravel in it, or paint the roof with white elastomeric paint. This shields the waterproof surface from the sun's heat.

Builders generally use the following application: one layer of 30-lb felt plus three layers of 15-lb felt plus the gravel.

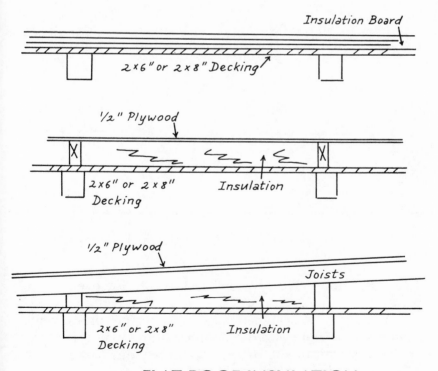

Figure 59. **FLAT ROOF INSULATION**

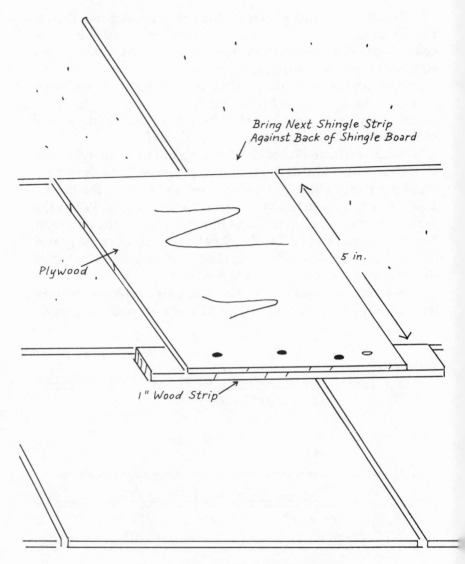

Figure 60. **SHINGLE BOARD**

This application will give satisfactory service over a long period of time.

You should install metal flashing wherever pipes, vents, conduits, or chimneys protrude through the roof (this is true of either flat or sloping roofs). You can buy this flashing from any building materials supply store.

Traditional Southwestern adobes also often use canales. These are metal-lined wooden troughs that extend through the wall to drain off the water from the roof.

If you intend to use asphalt shingles on a *sloping roof,* cover the rafters first with boards 1 inch (2.5 cm) thick and 6 to 8 inches (15–18 cm) wide, or ½ inch (1.3 cm) exterior plywood sheets, and lay the shingles directly over this.

Asphalt shingles (mineralized felt) have come a long way since the early days. There are currently many different types available, including the three-tab strip, T-lock shingles, two- and three-tab hexagon shingles, giant individual dutch lap shingles, and others. All come in a wide variety of colors and textures.

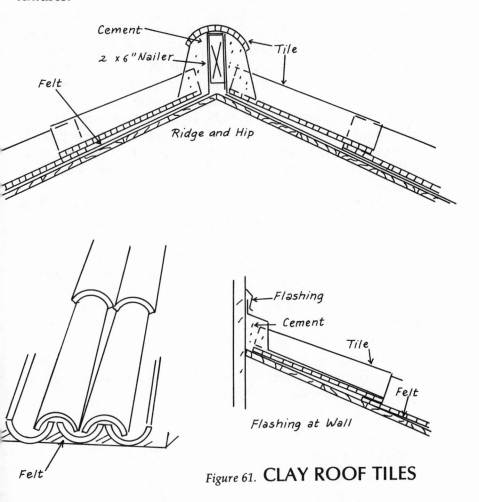

Figure 61. CLAY ROOF TILES

In covering the roof of an adobe house, you will find the three-tab, 36 inch by 12 inch (98 cm x 31 cm) strip the easiest to install. These shingles (as all others) are purchased in squares. One square equals 100 square feet (9.3 sq m) of roof surface.

The weight of asphalt shingles is also directly related to their life expectancy. Many manufacturers guarantee their 235-pound-per-square shingle for fifteen years, their 300- to 325-pound-per-square shingle for twenty years. Most roofers refer to asphalt shingles as fifteen-year shingles, twenty-year shingles, or whatever their life expectancy is.

To start laying asphalt shingles, first put down a strip of 15-pound asphalt felt from one side to the other, flush with the edge of the roof. Lay the next strip of asphalt felt in the same manner. However, when you lay the next strip of asphalt felt, overlap the first one by 2 to 6 inches (5–15 cm).

In laying the shingles, overlap the edge of the roof slightly with a double row of shingles (turn the bottom shingle upside down), or use a starter strip with a row of shingles nailed directly on top of it. Now lay the next row of shingles allowing a 5 inch (13 cm) overlap. You can keep the courses in line by snapping a chalk line across the roof, or you can make a 5 inch (13 cm) shingle board (Figure 60), which is laid over the preceding row.

When you reach a valley, simply continue across. This will give you a laced valley. Cap ridges and hips with single shingles nailed into place.

Wooden shingles and shakes are laid in a similar manner, except that ridges and hips are capped with a special capping shingle. Valleys are lined with metal flashing.

Clay tile also looks good with adobe. There are several types available including conventional mission tile, Lincoln tile (flat), Oriental tile (wavy), and others.

See Figure 61 for general methods of application. Check Infotile.com, and internet tile center. It features catalogs and installation information.

11
Finishing the Exterior
and Interior

Many very beautiful adobe houses achieve striking effects with exposed adobe bricks both inside and out. On the other hand, white plaster adobe houses roofed with Spanish tile are almost traditional in some areas, as are the flat-roofed Southwestern adobe houses.

APPLYING PLASTER

If you intend to plaster the exterior of your house, the first step is to nail an 18- or 20-gauge stucco mesh "chickenwire" to the outside of the house with 16-penny nails. The exact gauge used depends on your local code. This stucco mesh reinforces the plaster and helps bond it to the adobe.

Plaster is made with portland cement and lime. Proportions for mixing it are given below. For exterior walls, the plaster is applied ¾ inch (1.9 cm) thick in three coats (Figure 62). Apply the first coat, the *scratch coat*, with a flat trowel, then scratch or score that coat with a rake or a rakelike tool. Allow this scratch coat to dry one or two days before applying the second coat, the *brown coat*, ⅛ to ½ inch (.3–1.37 cm) thick with a trowel. Then compact and smooth the surface with a large wooden float (wooden trowel). You can buy or rent both types of trowels. The brown coat smooths the depressions left in the scratch coat.

Allow the brown coat to dry from seven to eleven days before applying the *final coat* (the color coat). In dry weather some builders shortcut the drying and apply the brown coat a few hours to a day after applying the scratch coat.

You can buy colored stucco for the color coat in ready-mixed colors or you can mix your own. Here are the proportions for the various exterior coats.

You can mix these materials in a wheelbarrow with a hoe, or in a powered plaster mixer. Apply the plaster using a hawk and a trowel. A hawk is a flat, square piece of aluminum that is used to carry mortar. Hawks often come with a detachable wooden handle and are available in sizes from 8 to 14 inches (20–36 cm). You can also use a square piece of plywood as a hawk if you prefer.

PLASTERING THE INTERIOR

When plastering inside, omit the stucco mesh and the scratch coat. First, apply a brown coat consisting of a mixture of 1

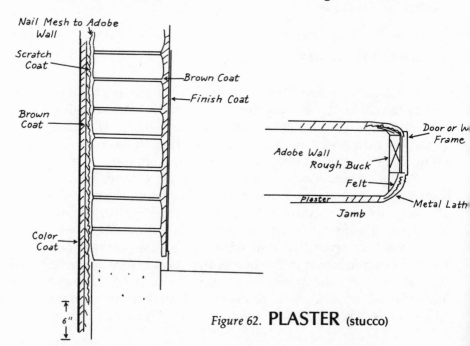

Figure 62. PLASTER (stucco)

Coat	Proportions
Scratch coat	1 bag portland cement ½ bag sack lime 8 #2 shovelfuls of sand
Brown coat	1 bag portland cement ½ bag sack lime 15 #2 shovelfuls sand
Color coat	4 sacks colored stucco ½ bag sack lime

sack of fibered plaster and 18 #2 shovelfuls of sand. After the brown coat dries, apply a finish coat that consists of 1 sack of unfibered plaster and 8 #2 shovelfuls of sand. Finish the masonry wall by water-brushing with a texture brush to smooth away trowel marks. You can buy these at some building supply stores. Fill the small holes and voids and remove any loose sand or grit. After drying check the wall surfaces for a tendency to chalk. If your hand shows a dusty coating, apply an additional finish coat. If it does not, apply a thin layer of texturing compound (bedding compound used in drywall work) obtainable from building supply stores or lumber yards. This powder should be mixed with water to a thick consistency and then brushed on. After it dries paint the surface any color you desire.

For detailed information on plastering consult the book *Plastering Skill and Practice*, F. Van Den Branden, Thomas L. Hartsell, American Technical Society.

INSTALLING DRYWALL

Drywall (sheetrock) is a mill-fabricated gypsum wallboard made with smooth, heavy paper on the face side and a strong paper backing. Sheetrock is the standard material used today for covering interior frame walls. The 4 by 8 foot (1.2 x 2.4 m) sheets are butted together and nailed to the studs. The edges of the sheet will fall at the center of the studs for walls constructed of studs placed on 16 inch (41 cm) centers. You will have to cut the last sheet in each wall to fit.

After the sheets are nailed in place, you must tape them with perforated drywall tape. First, apply a smooth layer of drywall bedding compound to the joint using a 6 inch (15 cm) broad knife. Then place perforated drywall tape over this and smooth the tape out with a knife. Also smooth out all nail holes with bedding compound. Let the compound dry overnight, then apply bedding compound over the tape. Try to make the joints as smooth as possible. After you have allowed this coat to dry overnight, sand the joints and apply a thin mix of drywall texturing (bedding compound). When this dries paint with a roller or brush.

If you prefer to use paneling instead of sheetrock, you can buy it in sheets the same size as the sheetrock. You will find a wide variety from which to choose at any building materials supply store. Rough exterior plywood paneling also makes an attractive finish along with the adobe. Install by nailing in place as you did the sheetrock. Cut the sheets to fit at the end of each wall and cut holes for any electrical outlets or switches.

SELECTING AND HANGING DOORS

You can choose between standard swing doors (the common door), pocket doors (a door that slips sideways into a wall opening), bi-fold doors (doors that fold in the middle), and sliding bypass doors (two doors that slide past each other).

The pocket door is used when you don't have enough space inside the room to open a regular door. The sliding bypass and folding doors are primarily used as easy-access doors for long closets and pantries or to close off two rooms.

Hollow-core doors, which are used for most interior door installations, have a layer of plywood on both sides and a hollow core usually reinforced with honeycomb cardboard. These doors are lightweight and relatively inexpensive, and resist warping well.

Solid-core doors generally have a solid interior of flakeboard or inexpensive plywood with a layer of plywood over either side. Use solid-core doors in all exterior locations.

Most interior doors are flush—that is, they are completely smooth on both sides. Adobe builders, however, usually utilize some type of paneled door for the front entrance. The most economical panel doors have thin plywood panels. Panel doors are also available with a wide variety of raised panels and some very striking designs. You can create a very unusual and handsome front entrance with ornate hand-carved doors, which are quite expensive but worth it when you are trying to create a special effect.

The standard height for a house door is 6 feet 8 inches (2 m); for a garage door, 7 feet (2.1 m). The widths of standard doors vary with their use.

Standard Door Widths

Use	Width	Thickness
Bathrooms	2 ft 0 in	1⅜ in
Bedrooms	2 ft 4 in to 2 ft 6 in	1⅜ in
Back doors	2 ft 8 in	1¾ in
Front entrances	3 ft 0 in	1¾ in

All doors fasten directly to a doorframe consisting of finished side and head jambs (side and top pieces) made from ¾ inch (1.9 cm) stock of varying widths (1 × 4 or 1 × 6). You can make these frames or you can buy them ready-made. You can also buy prefabricated factory-assembled units in which the door is hung, fitted, and locked in the frame.

To install the doorframe (figure 63), place the assembled frame in the rough opening and hold it in place temporarily with nails. To keep the side jambs properly spaced, place a spreader (a piece of lumber the width of the frame) between the jambs on the floor. At this point, using a carpenter's level, level one side of the frame. Place shims or a pieces of shingle at the top and bottom to provide a backing, then nail with 8-penny finishing nails.

Next, using a straightedge, align the back by inserting pieces of shingle behind the frame as shown. Nail in place with 8-penny finishing nails. Level and straighten the other side in the same manner. Make sure you place extra shims behind the hinge areas to provide a solid backing for the hinges. Finally, place shims behind the top frame member (head jamb) and nail in place with 8-penny nails (Figure 64).

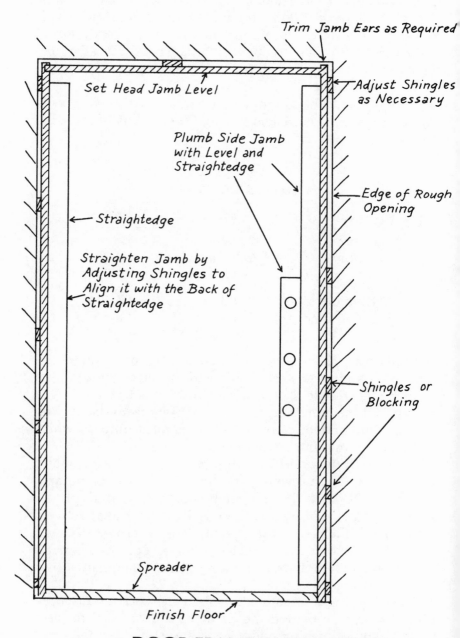

Trim Jamb Ears as Required

Set Head Jamb Level

Adjust Shingles as Necessary

Plumb Side Jamb with Level and Straightedge

Edge of Rough Opening

Straightedge

Straighten Jamb by Adjusting Shingles to Align it with the Back of Straightedge

Shingles or Blocking

Spreader

Finish Floor

Figure 63. **DOOR FRAME INSTALLATION**

On each frame you will need to provide stops, small strips usually made from ½ inch (1.3 cm) stock, which are nailed to the frame to prevent the door from swinging through the opening. Usually exterior frames are milled, or run through a router, to remove a notch that acts as the stop.

On exterior doors you must also install some type of wooden or metal sill. These sills come in varying heights to allow for the differences in thickness of carpet, tile, or other floor covering.

Finally, you will need to install casings. These are finished, milled pieces of lumber that cover the joints between the frame and the wall. Casings are available from a lumber yard or building materials dealer in a wide variety of patterns. In an adobe house, rectangular pieces of stained, finish, or rough lumber blend well with either plastered walls or exposed adobe.

Some builders draw up a separate door schedule that they include with the plans. This schedule shows the size and

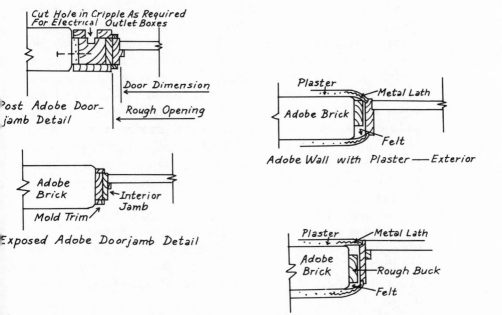

Figure 64. TYPICAL ADOBE DOORJAMB DETAIL

type of door, the frame and hardware, and any special specifications. In most cases, however, building departments will allow you to mark the door sizes and any other information right on your floor plan instead of making a separate door-schedule box.

INSTALLING THE WINDOWS

You have a choice of three basic types of windows: sliding, swinging, or fixed.

Double-hung sliding windows slide up and down past each other and are held in position by counterweights or stops. *Horizontal sliding windows* slide past each other in a horizontal direction on top and bottom tracks. Modern horizontal sliding windows are preglazed (the glass is sealed in place) and are made with aluminum frames.

Casement windows are hinged on the side to swing out. They are usually operated by a crank or lever. Screens for these windows are placed inside the room. *Awning windows* are top-pivoted and open outward from the bottom. Screens are mounted inside. *Hopper windows* are bottom-pivoted and open inward from the top. *Fixed windows* do not open but are useful where you have a large window space along one wall or where a good view is the major consideration. Fixed windows are often combined with operating windows or with a sliding glass door in a wide variety of arrangements.

Most manufactured windows come with the sash, frame, glass, and all the hardware. If you buy your windows from a local dealer, that dealer may install the windows as part of the purchase price.

In general, windows are rough-framed to the dimensions marked on your plans. Each manufacturer, however, makes windows to slightly different specifications. In order to make rough openings the correct size you should select your windows in advance and rough-frame to the manufacturer's specifications.

Andersen Corporation, Bayport, Minn. 55003, for instance, provides a table of sizes for each window type it manufactures. The Andersen gliding windows are rough-framed to such predetermined sizes as 30½ by 30½ inches (77.5

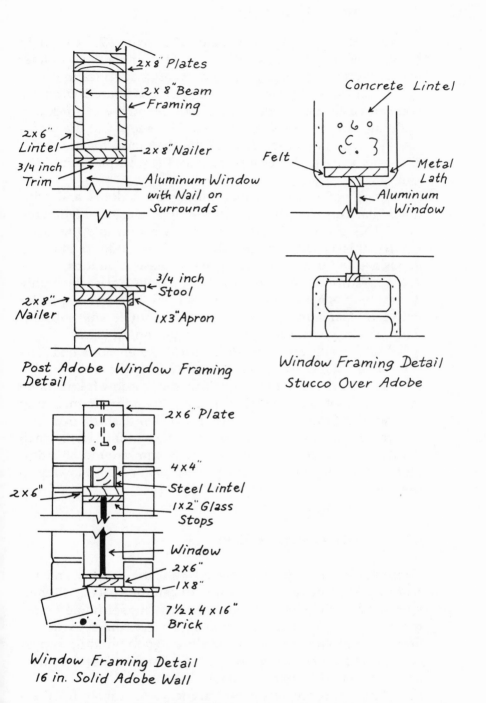

2 x 8" Plates

2 x 8" Beam
Framing

2 x 6"
Lintel

2 x 8" Nailer

3/4 inch
Trim

Aluminum Window
with Nail on
Surrounds

3/4 inch
Stool

2 x 8"
Nailer

1 x 3" Apron

**Post Adobe Window Framing
Detail**

Concrete Lintel

Felt

Metal
Lath

Aluminum
Window

**Window Framing Detail
Stucco Over Adobe**

2 x 6" Plate

4 x 4"
Steel Lintel

2 x 6"

1 x 2" Glass
Stops

Window

2 x 6"

1 x 8"

7½ x 4 x 16"
Brick

**Window Framing Detail
16 in. Solid Adobe Wall**

Figure 65. **WINDOW SECTIONS**

cm × 77.5 cm), 36½ by 30½ inches (92.7 cm × 77.5 cm), 36½ by 40½ inches (92.7 cm × 102.9 cm), and similar sizes. Other manufacturers offer similar rough opening specifications.

If you would prefer not to buy manufactured windows you can easily make your own. You can buy sash stock at a building materials dealer or from a door shop. Cut the pieces at a 45° angle in a miter box and put the pieces together with glue and screws. Use clamps to hold them in place until the glue dries.

Some codes require that sliding glass doors and windows that come all the way to the floor must use tempered glass. This prevents injury to anyone walking into the glass. Even if this is not required by your local code, it is still a good idea to install tempered glass in these situations.

In addition, in cold climates insulated glass is highly desirable. It is made of two layers of glass with an air space in between. Insulating glass is expensive but it will substantially reduce your heating and air conditioning losses.

Windowsills can be made of brick, cement, or wood. The exterior sill slopes to carry water away from the wall.

Install your windows by nailing the window frame to the rough buck or to the rough post adobe window frame. After the frame is firmly in place, install wooden flashing trim.

If you are installing an aluminum window frame, nail the frame in place, then nail the finish trim around all sides. Place facing material over this to keep water from blowing in the joints.

INSTALLING KITCHEN CABINETS

Cabinets are an important part of both the kitchen and the bathrooms. Initially, try to plan your cabinet space to fit your needs. You might want to look through model homes, then modify the cabinet arrangements you see there to fit the house you intend to build. In addition, go to building supply stores that feature ready-made cabinets and look at the many styles and combinations available.

When you are ready for cabinets you can build them yourself, or hire a local cabinetmaker to manufacture them for you; or you can buy ready-made cabinets from a number of building supply and mail-order firms.

Typical kitchen cabinets are made with a 36 inch (91 cm) high, 24 inch (70 cm) deep base cabinet and a 30 to 32 inch (78–83 cm) high, 12 inch (31 cm) deep wall cabinet, with doors of plywood, pressed hardboard, or hardwood veneer over plywood. You can order your cabinets prefinished or you can paint or stain them yourself.

Most cabinet counters are plastic laminate (such as Formica) that are stain-resistant and come in a variety of patterns or colors. You can install these tops yourself or have a cabinetmaker do it.

To install a plastic laminate counter, glue the plastic laminate to a sheet of plywood with contact cement. Brush the cement on the pieces to be glued, allow to dry, then press the pieces together.

The easiest way to anchor wall cabinets to an adobe wall is to screw them directly into the adobe, or provide nailer strips between the adobes. You can do this when you lay up the wall. You can also do drill holes and insert large wooden dowels. Or you can build a frame wall directly in front of the adobe wall and anchor the cabinets to this.

In a post adobe house you can nail anchor boards across the posts and secure the cabinets to these. The face frame of a cabinet usually projects at least one inch on either side; close the gaps here with a piece of millwork trim.

Before the wall cabinets are fastened to the wall, they are usually held in place on temporary supports such as specially built sawhorses. Trim the cabinets if necessary to fit the wall, then fasten into place with nails or screws through the backing strip.

You will need to level the base cabinets in both directions, then adjust for level with wooden shim shingles. Again, fasten this cabinet to the wall by nailing through the top rail.

SELECTING AND INSTALLING FLOOR COVERING

Adobe houses, as already discussed, are generally built on either a concrete slab or on a concrete or concrete block foundation with a wooden floor. On a concrete slab you can install either carpet, vinyl tile, or tile. On a wooden floor you can install hardwood, vinyl tile, or carpet.

Wooden floors consist of two parts, the subfloor and the final finish flooring. The subfloor is usually installed by nailing 1 × 8 boards diagonally to the joists or by putting down ⅜ to ½ inch (.95 to 1.3 cm) plywood. Nail the subfloor in place with 8-penny cement-coated nails. If you intend to carpet or to install vinyl tile, nail ½ inch (1.3 cm) particleboard over this.

If you intend to finish with hardwood, you will find a wide variety of prefinished or unfinished hardwood flooring available. Because of the difficulty in finishing hardwood I highly recommend that you buy it in a prefinished state. Most hardwood flooring is tongue-and-grooved. Simply nail it directly to the subflooring by toenailing through the groove.

When it comes to selecting carpeting, it is best to have samples brought to the house rather than to try to make your selection in the store. Since most adobe houses have a very special look, what looked striking in the store may look quite bland when placed next to an adobe wall. Usually the price of the installation is not included in the price of the carpet.

Vinyl floor tile also makes a good floor covering in an adobe house, especially in the bathrooms and kitchen. Before laying the tile you should first prepare the floor. If you have nailed particleboard directly over wooden subflooring, make sure the nails are flush and all the larger holes are filled. You should also sand down any rough joints to make sure they are smooth and flush. Before actually applying the tile, you will want to seal the particleboard with a latex floor and wax primer. On concrete, remove any bumps with a chisel, then apply the latex floor and wax primer.

To lay the tiles you can use a vinyl tile adhesive or buy self-sticking tiles. Divide the floor into four sections, then start from the center line and lay your tiles outward to the edge. Plan the starting point so that you will end with equal portions of tile on all sides, as opposed to half a tile on one side and a small sliver on the other. Do this by laying tile pieces (without adhesive) in both directions to the edge. When you have the arrangement you want, simply adjust the starting point.

Actually, ceramic tile probably looks better with adobe than does almost any other type of floor covering. You can buy quarry tile, precast colored and patterned concrete tile, terrazzo (cement, sand, and marble chips), ceramic mosaic tile, glazed tile, and other types.

Before laying the tile, soak it overnight in water so that it becomes wet all the way through. Next spread a damp mix of 1 part portland cement and 4 parts sand on your pre-dampened concrete slab. Smooth this mixture with a screed (as we did when pouring the original concrete slab in Chapter 4).

Place the tile on top of this "thin set" mix and gently tap in with a rubber hammer. Use the same mix for mortar between the tile joints. To prevent the concrete from curing too fast, dampen the joints and keep them damp for a day or two.

You can clean the tile as you go along or clean it later with muriatic (hydrochloric) acid. Lay the tile using the same center line procedure as for vinyl tile above.

ADDING THE TRIM

With a post adobe house you will usually want to add a fascia board at the top of the wall inside to cover the rough header boards. The fascia can be finished or rough 1 × 10s or 1 × 12s stained to any color you desire. It is also possible to stain the rough header boards with a dark opaque stain and leave them as part of the house.

Interior frame walls are usually trimmed with a base trim. There are many baseboard patterns available or you can simply use a 1 × 2 or similar size piece of lumber and stain it to match your decor. If you have built a post adobe you will probably want to stain all exposed lumber surfaces some shade of dark brown.

Stains come either clear or opaque depending on the surface to which they are to be applied. Although I like to bring out the wood grain, I find that I always do better using opaque stain. Drywall can be painted any color you desire.

Plain or fancy door hardware and similar trim will add to the appearance of your house. A wide variety of types and styles are available. Before making a selection it is a good idea to visit several building supply stores to see what choices you actually have. In many cases these dealers have several manufacturers' catalogs from which you can special-order.

Finally, I have discovered from experience that you never actually finish an adobe house. As you live in it you will always find something more that you want to do to make it more complete, such as adding fancy lighting fixtures, or raising the living room ceiling to install beams, or adding more windows, or a hundred-and-one other things.

An adobe house actually seems to become almost a living entity, and, as thousands before me have discovered, living in one for any length of time can easily make you an adobe addict for life.

Bibliography

BOOKS ON ADOBE

Adobe Architecture
Myrtle Stedman
and Wilfred Stedman
  Sunstone Press
  Box 2321
  Santa Fe, NM 87504, 1987

Adobe: Build It Yourself
Paul Graham McHenry, Jr.
  University of Arizona Press
  1230 Park Ave.
  Tucson, AZ 85719, 1985

Adobe: Building and Living with Earth
Orlando Romero, David Larkin,
Michael Freeman
  Houghton Mifflin Company
  222 Berkeley St.
  Boston, MA 02116, 1994

Adobe and Rammed Earth Building:
Design and Construction
Paul Graham McHenry, Jr.
  University of Arizona Press
  1230 Park Ave.
  Tucson, AZ 85719, 1989

Adobe: Remodeling and Fireplaces
Myrtle Stedman
  Sunstone Press
  Box 2321
  Santa Fe, NM 87504, 1986

The Adobe Story: A Global Treasure
Paul Graham McHenry, Jr.
  University of New Mexico Press
  1720 Lomas Blvd. NE
  Albuquerque, NM 87131,
  1998 and 2000

Adobe! Homes and Interiors of Taos
and Santa Fe and the Southwest
Sandy Seth, Sandra Seth, Laurel Seth
  Architectural Book Publishing Co.
  268 Dogwood Lane
  Stamford, CT 06903, 1998

Ageless Adobe: History and Preservation
in Southwestern Architecture
Jerome Iowa
  Sunstone Press
  Box 2321
  Santa Fe, NM 87504, 1985

Build with Adobe
Marcia Southwick
  Swallow Press
  Ohio University Press
  Athens, OH 45701, 1994

New Mexico Style: A Sourcebook
of Traditional Architectural Details
Nancy Hunter Warren,
William Lumpkins
  Museum of New Mexico Press
  Box 2087
  Santa Fe, NM 87504, 1995

Spectacular Vernacular:
The Adobe Tradition
Jean-Louis Bourgeois
  Aperture
  20 East 23rd St.
  New York, NY 10010, 1990

Southwest Home Plans:
138 Sun-Loving Designs
  Home Planners, Inc.
  3275 West Ina Rd., Suite 110
  Tucson, AZ 85741, 1996

BOOKS ON SOLAR HEATING

*Designing and Building a Solar
House, Your Place in the Sun*
Donald Watson
   Garden Way Publishing Co.
   Charlotte, Vt. 05445, 1977

Handbook of Homemade Power.
Mother Earth News
Bantam Books
666 Fifth Ave.
New York, N.Y. 10019, 1974

Homegrown Sundwellings
Peter Van Dresser
   Lightning Tree Publications,
   P.O. Box 1837
   Santa Fe, N.M. 87501, 1978

How to Build a Solar Heater
Ted Lucas
   Ward Ritchie Press
   Pasadena, Calif. 91100, 1975

*Low Cost Energy Efficient Shelter
for the Owner and Builder*
Eugene Eccli
   Rodale Press, Emmaus, Pa.
   18049 1975

*New Low Cost Sources of Energy
for the Home*
Peter Clegg
   Garden Way Publishing Co.,
   Charlotte, Vt. 05445, 1977

Producing Your Own Power
Carol Hupping Stoner, ed.
   Vintage Books
   201 E. 50th St.
   New York, N.Y. 10022, 1974

Solar Age Catalog
   Solar Vision Inc.
   200 E. Main St.
   Port Jervis, N.Y. 13771, 1976

Solar Dwelling Design Concepts
AIA Research Corporation,
Superintendent of Documents,
Washington, D.C. 20402, 1976

The Solar Greenhouse Book
James C. McCullagh, ed.
Rodale Press
Emmaus, Pa. 18049, 1978

*The Food and Heat Producing
Solar Greenhouse: Design,
Construction and Operation*
Rick Fisher and Bill Yanda
John Muir Publications
P.O. Box 613
Santa Fe, N.M. 87501, 1976

*Solar Heated Buildings:
A Brief Survey*
W. A. Shurcliff
   19 Appleton St.
   Cambridge, Mass. 02138
   1977

*Solar Heating and
Cooling Engineering:
Practical Design and Economics*
Jan Kreider and Frank Kreith
   McGraw-Hill Book Co., 1976

The Solar Home Book
Bruce Anderson
   Cheshire Books
   Church Hill
   Harrisville, N.H. 03450, 1976

Solar Homes and Sun Heating
George Daniels
   Harper & Row
   10 E. 53rd St.
   New York, N.Y. 10022, 1976

*Sunset Homeowners Guide
to Solar Heating*
   Lane Publishing Co.
   Menlo Park
   Calif. 94025, 1978

Index

access road
  costs of, 10–11
  easement for, 11
adobe brick(s)
  contents of, 35–36
    emulsified asphalt in, 37–38
    portland cement in, 38
  dimensions of, 40, 63
  kiln-fired, 38
  laying of, 61–63, 62 (fig.)
  from machine presses, 41
  part-bricks, 44, 46
  soil test for, 11–13
  storage of, 46, 47 (fig.), 48
  strength tests of, 38–39
  Uniform Building Code on, 36
adobe brickmaking
  drying procedures in, 44, 46, 47
    (fig.)
  machine presses for, 41
  mixing methods in, 42–43
  molds for, 40–41, 40 (fig.)
    cleaning of, 44, 46 (fig.)
  output in, 48
  pouring and smoothing steps in,
    44, 45 (fig.)
  surface for, 42

adobe construction
  cabinet installation in, 150–51
  doors in, 144–48
  drywall in, 143–44
  of fireplace, 117–26
  floor covering in, 151–53
  foundation in, 32–33, 49–59
  geographical range of, 2
  interior trim for, 153–54
  materials for, 153–54
  materials for, 2–3
  plastering in, 141–43
  roof in, 127–40
  walls in, 60–76
  windows in, 148–50, 149 (fig.)
  See also post adobe construction
adobe house(s)
  construction costs of, 1, 2
  cooling system for, 115–16
  drainage system for, 77–84
  electrical wiring of, 90–105
  heating system of, 106–15
  plans for, 20–34
    drawing up of, 30–34
    of garage, 28
    of kitchen-utility area, 22, 24, 25
      (fig.), 26

adobe house(s), plans for (*cont.*)
  of living area, 20–22, 23
  permits and inspection of, 34
  of sleeping area, 26–28
  storage in, 29–30
  septic system of, 88–89
  site selection of, 4–17
    access roads in, 10–11
    power and telephone lines in, 9–10
    price in, 16–17
    road construction plans and, 14
    septic tank percolation in, 7–8
    soil content in, 11–13
    terrain in, 16
    title check and, 14–16
    water potential in, 4–7
    zoning law and, 13–14
  styles of, 18–20, 19 (fig.)
  water supply system in, 84–88
air conditioning
  central, 115–16
  single unit, 115
  wiring for, 101
appliances, electrical wiring of, 99–101 (fig.), 102 (fig.)
asphalt, emulsified, 35–36
  in brickmaking, 37–38
asphalt shingle roof, 138 (fig.), 139–40

baseboard heating, 112
baseboard trim, 153
bathroom fixtures
  drainage system for, 82–84
  frame for, 84, 85 (fig.)
  installation of, 87–88
  water supply lines to, 86–87
bathroom plan, 26–28
  storage in, 29
bathtub
  connection of, 88
  drainage from, 78, 81–83
  frame for, 84
  water supply lines to, 86
beams, 129, 130
bedroom plan, 26–27, 28
  storage in, 29
bi-fold doors, 144

bond beams, 65–66, 65 (fig.)
Boudreau, Eugene, 2
breaker box. *See* service panel
brickmaking. *See* adobe brickmaking

canales, 139
carpeting, selection of, 152
casement windows, 148
casings, 147
ceiling joists, 129, 130–31
  on gable roof, 131–32
ceiling register, 110
ceramic tile, installation of, 152–53
chimney(s)
  construction of, 125–26
  plans for, 121 (fig.), 122 (fig.)
CINVA Ram, 41
circuits, 93–95, 94 (fig.)
  labeling of, 105
  testing of, 104–5
  wiring of, 96–97
clay roof tiles, 139 (fig.), 140
clay soil, for adobe bricks, 11–13, 35
concrete piers, 58
concrete slab, 53 (fig.)
  drainage system and, 77
  floor coverings for, 151
  footings for, 52–54
  pouring of, 55, 56–57
    tools in, 57 (fig.)
  water supply system and, 86–87
conduit
  installation of, 98–99
  size of, 99
connectors, twist-on solderless, 97–99, 98 (fig.)
cooling systems, 115–16
copper wire
  capacity of, 92, 93
  size of, 91–92, 93
corbelling of bricks, 123–24
corner staking, 50, 51 (fig.), 52
Counterflow furnace, 106–7, 107 (fig.)

damper, installation of, 123
den plan, 22, 23
dining room plan, 21, 23

dishwasher
    installation of, 87
    water supply lines to, 86
door(s)
    hardware for, 153–54
    installation of, 145–47
    lintels for, 66, 67 (fig.)
    plan of, 147–48
    in post adobe construction, 74
    rough buck frame for, 63–65
    standard height and width of, 145
    types of, 144
doorframe, 145–47, 146 (fig.)
doorjamb, 147 (fig.)
drafting basics, for adobe house
        plan, 30–34, 31 (fig.)
drainage system
    drain plan for, 79
    installation of, 82–84, 83 (fig.)
    plastic pipe for, 80 (fig.)
        cutting and fitting of, 82
        size of, 80–81
    revent pipes in, 78
    stacks of, 77–78
    trench preparation for, 81–82
dryer, wiring of, 101
drywall
    finish on, 153
    installation of, 143–44
ductwork
    installation of, 110–11
    insulation of, 111–12, 111 (fig.)
    systems of, 108, 109 (fig.)

earthquake areas, steel reinforced
        walls in, 66
electrical outlets, placement of, 90–91
electrical wiring
    of circuits, 93–95, 94 (fig.), 97
        testing and labeling in, 104–5
    conduit installation in, 98–99
    connectors in, 97, 98 (fig.)
    of heavy-duty appliances, 99–101,
        101 (fig.), 102 (fig.)
    information sources on, 90
    plan of, 90–91
        symbols on, 92 (fig.)
    of receptacle box, 95, 97

of service panel, 102–3, 104 (fig.)
    wire and box selection for, 91–93,
        95–96
elevation sheet, on house plan, 33
equipment and tools
    for brickmaking, 42
    for concrete slab construction, 57
        (fig.)
    for wall construction, 60
evaporative cooler, 115

family room plan, 21–22, 23
fascia board trim, 153
fiberboard roof decking, 136
firebox, 123
fireplace(s)
    circulating, 126
    foundations for, 52–53, 120
        construction of, 120–26
    information sources on, 119
    opening size for, 119–20
        flue liner and, 124
    plans for, 120, 121 (fig.), 122 (fig.)
    types of, 117–18
fixed windows, 148
flat roof, 127
    cover for, 136
    framing of, 130–31
floor(s)
    coverings for, 151–53
    wood frame foundation for, 57–58,
        58 (fig.)
    joist span in, 59
floor plan, 32
floor register, 110
flue liner, size of, 124
folding doors, 144
footings
    concrete for, 53–54
    depth of, 52
    dimensions of, 52
    trenches for, 53
forced-air heating, 106–12
foundation
    of concrete block wall, 53 (fig.),
        54–55
    of concrete slab, 53 (fig.), 55–57
    corner-staking for, 50, 51 (fig.), 52

foundation (*continued*)
  footings of, 52–54
  grade determination for, 49–50, 51
    (fig.)
  plan of, 32–33
  wood floor frame in, 57–58, 58 (fig.)
front entrance, 22
Full Length Rafter Framer Book, The,
    132–33, 136
furnace
  capacity of, 108
  Counterflow, 106–7, 107 (fig.)
  installation of, 108–12
fuse box. *See* service panel

gable roof, 127
  framing of, 131–33, 134
garage plan, 28
  storage in, 29
girders, in floor frame, 57, 58 (fig.), 59
grade elevation, determination of,
    49–50, 51 (fig.)

hardwood floor, 152
Hartsell, Thomas L., 143
header beam, in post adobe construc-
    tion, 71–74, 72–73 (fig.)
hearth, 126
heating system
  forced-air, 106–12
  radiant, 112
  solar, 114–15
hip roof, 127
  framing of, 135–36
hollow-core doors, 144
hopper windows, 148

joists
  ceiling, 129, 130–31
    on gable roof, 131–32
  floor, 57–58
    spans for, 59

kitchen
  cabinet installation in, 150–51
  electrical outlets in, 91
  lighting units in, 91
  plan of, 22, 24, 25 (fig.), 26
  storage in, 29

kitchen fixtures
  installation of, 87–88
  water supply lines to, 86–87
Kiva fireplace, 118, 119 (fig.)

latilla, 137
library plan, 22, 23
lighting
  fixture selection for, 97
  plan for, 91
lintels, 66, 67 (fig.)
living room plan, 20–21, 23

Making the Adobe Brick (Boudreau), 2
molds
  cleaning of, 44, 46 (fig.)
  construction of, 40–41
mortar, formula for, 60–61
mud sill, 58

National Electrical Code, 90

office plan, 22, 23

paneling, of interior walls, 144
percolation test, of septic system, 7–8
plastering
  exterior, 141–42
  interior, 142–43
Plastering Skill and Practice (Van Den
    Branden), 143
plaster mixer, in brickmaking, 42–43,
    43 (fig.)
plot plan, 32
plumbing system
  drainage in, 77–84
  water supply in, 84–88
plywood paneling, for interior walls,
    144
pocket doors, 144
post adobe construction
  cabinet installation in, 151
  door and window framing in, 74
  electrical wiring in, 95, 96 (fig.), 98
  headers and top plates in, 71–74,
    72–73 (fig.)
  interior walls in, 75
  trim for, 153

post holders for, 68, 70 (fig.), 71
posts and frames for, 68
roof in, 131 (fig.)
post holders, placement of, 68–71, 70
(fig.), 71 (fig.)
power lines, extension of, 9–10

radiant heating, 112
rafter(s)
hip, 135
jack, 136
layout of, 132, 133–35, 134 (fig.)
measurements for, 132–33
spans for, 129
valley, 136
range, electrical wiring of, 99, 101
(fig.)
receptacle box
installation of, 95
wiring of, 97
recreation room plan, 21–22, 23
register outlets
location of, 108
types of, 110
revent pipes, 78
ridgeboard, 131–32
roof
covering of, 136–40
framing of, 33, 130–36
plan of, 128–30
span tables for, 129, 130
styles of, 127–28
waterproofing of, 137–38
rough buck frame, 63–65, 64 (fig.)

San Valle Tile Kilns, The, 140
septic system
construction of, 88–89
percolation test for, 7–8
size of, 88
service panel, 93
installation of, 102–3, 104 (fig.)
shed roof, 127
sheetrock, installation of, 143–44
shingleboard roof, 138 (fig.), 139–40
shower(s)
connection of, 88
drainage for, 78, 81, 83

frames for, 84, 85 (fig.)
water supply lines to, 86
sills
door, 147
window, 150
sink
installation of, 87
water supply lines to, 86
sliding doors, 144, 150
sliding windows, 148
sloping roof, asphalt shingles on, 138
(fig.), 139–40
smoke chamber, fireplace, 123–24
soil content, in adobe bricks, 11–13
soil stack, 77–78
solar heating, 114–15
solid-core doors, 144
Southwest adobes, 18–20, 19 (fig.)
stain, for interior trim, 153
steel reinforcing bars, 66–67
storage area, plan of, 29–30
story pole, 61
stove. See range
straw, in adobe bricks, 35
string guides, for adobe walls, 61, 62
(fig.)
Strout Realty catalog, 16
stucco, application of, 141–42, 142
(fig.)
stud wall, interior, 75–76, 75 (fig.)
swing doors, 144
switches
in electrical plan, 91
types of, 97
wiring of, 100 (fig.)

telephone lines, extension of, 9–10
tile floors, installation of, 152–53
title check, 14–16
toilet
drainage from, 82–83
installation of, 87–88
water supply lines to, 86
tools. See equipment and tools

Uniform Building Code, on adobe
brick, 36

United Farm Agency catalog, 16
utility room plan, 24, 26

Van Den Branden, F., 143
vigas, 129, 130, 131
vinyl floor tile, installation of, 152

wall construction
  bond beams in, 65–66, 65 (fig.)
  bricklaying in, 61–63, 62 (fig.)
  equipment for, 60
  interior, 75–76, 75 (fig.)
  lintels in, 66, 67 (fig.)
  mortar for, 60–61
  in post adobe house, 68–76, 69
    (fig.), 70 (fig.)
  rough buck frame in, 63–65, 64
    (fig.)
  steel reinforcing rods in, 66–67
warm air outlets, installation of, 109
washer, water supply lines to, 86
water heater
  placement of, 84–85
  size recommendation for, 85
  wiring of, 101, 102 (fig.)
water rights, information on, 15

water supply
  from existing wells, 5–6
  information sources on, 4–5
  from surface springs, 5
  location of, 6–7
water supply system(s)
  fixture installation in, 87–88
  pipe connections in, 86–87
  pipe size for, 86
  plan for, 84–85
well(s)
  flow rate of, 5–6
  water location for, 6–7
window(s)
  dimensions of, 148, 150
  glass for, 150
  installation of, 150
  lintels for, 66, 67 (fig.)
  in post adobe construction, 74
  rough buck frames for, 63–65, 64
    (fig.)
  sills for, 150
  types of, 148
wood floor, coverings for, 151–52
wood frame walls, 75–76
wood shingles, 140

zoning law, and site selection, 13–14